T0384031

Managing Workplace Substance Misuse

This book provides professionals with the confidence and know-how to build a complete substance misuse management programme and deliver it within their respective workplace, regardless of sector or discipline.

Organizations are frequently in the dark about their rights and obligations where substance misuse takes place in their workplace, affects performance or employee wellbeing, or in extreme cases has a devastating impact on both the company and its employees. There is no formal training for HR, occupational health or health & safety professionals, solicitors, union representatives and many other professions. This book is written to help those professions, as well as individuals, understand the step-by-step process for building a complete workplace substance and alcohol misuse programme.

Managing Workplace Substance Misuse is written by the UK's only registered expert witness for substance misuse policy writing, implementation and mediation. With decades of expertise and first-hand experience of implementing effective policies in some of the UK's and world's biggest organizations, Trevor Hall helps organizations navigate this complex problem, offering consultancy advice and a roadmap to policy development and its implementation, providing you with a comprehensive consultancy in one volume. He explains, too, the central role industry and commerce play in the identification of substance misuse and the rehabilitation of staff, as well as what organizations can do to protect themselves from the culpability of getting things wrong in a litigious society.

Trevor Hall is the co-founder of Hall & Angus, a CPD-accredited consultancy and training provider specializing in workplace substance misuse management. Trevor has over 50 years' experience in substance misuse management and the enforcement of law in the area. In that capacity he has reviewed hundreds of workplace substance misuse policies and has written hundreds of policies across numerous countries. He also designed and built a 10,000-sq. ft. UKAS-accredited workplace-dedicated toxicology lab. Many of the principles applied globally are exhibited in the book and have been tried and tested by Trevor over the last 25 years in many sectors of commerce and industry.

Managing Workplace Substance Misuse

A Guide for Professionals

Trevor Hall

Routledge
Taylor & Francis Group

LONDON AND NEW YORK

First published 2020
by Routledge
2 Park Square, Milton Park, Abingdon, Oxon OX14 4RN

and by Routledge
52 Vanderbilt Avenue, New York, NY 10017

Routledge is an imprint of the Taylor & Francis Group, an informa business

British Library Cataloguing-in-Publication Data
A catalogue record for this book is available from the British Library

Library of Congress Cataloging-in-Publication Data
A catalog record has been requested for this book

ISBN: 978-0-367-24359-3 (hbk)
ISBN: 978-0-429-28200-3 (ebk)

Typeset in Optima
by Deanta Global Publishing Services, Chennai, India.

Contents

Some common drugs found in the workplace

(a) (b)

There are three types of cannabis you could expect to encounter in the workplace. Most cannabis will be smoked, but it can also be consumed in other preparations. The two pictures here show the cannabis hybrid called skunk. It can be as high as 40% in tetrahydrocannabinol (THC). In the 1960s cannabis sativa was as low as 4% in THC. Modern hybrid cannabis can be hallucinogenic and cause psychotic mental health episodes.

Pictures of cannabis plants being cultivated illegally in a hydroponics operation at an unoccupied building where the electricity supply had been illegally accessed.

Picture of cannabis drying and prepared for smoking in an unoccupied dwelling where the electricity supply had been illegally connected.

Picture of dried cannabis secreted in a confectionary toy container kept by the user in clothing, vehicles, lockers, bags, etc.

The first two pictures show possible drug preparations of personal use cannabis bush and cannabis resin for smoking (courtesy of Martin Vickerman). Employees may have this in their possession in the workplace, bags, lockers, etc. or in their vehicles on the employer's property. Be sure you know what you are looking for.

The third picture shows some paraphernalia of cannabis bush users who need to grind the dried leaf to prepare it for smoking in a pipe bong or reefer (joint). In the UK grinders are legal to purchase, as are the pipes, bongs and other drug paraphernalia as in the top left picture. Are they legal to buy or manufacture in your country?

The above picture (courtesy of Martin Vickerman) shows the other two preparations of cannabis and a cannabis mesh pipe. The large kilo brick is of cannabis resin (sticky crystal deposits), obtained from the fresh undried leaf, stems and flowers of the cannabis plant. Resin is generally stronger than cannabis bush. Also shown is a king ball of resin where producers rub cannabis plants in their hand to retrieve the resin which they then roll into a ball. The more proficient producers can use many methods of producing cannabis and cannabis dust from dried plants, etc.
The small bottle contains the strongest type of cannabis, which is cannabis (hash) oil. This is obtained by pressing the resin and some other preparation to recover the strongest cannabis oil, which can be 60–90% pure hash oil. The oil is generally brushed down the side of a cigarette and smoked. Cannabis is often considered a gateway drug to other drugs.

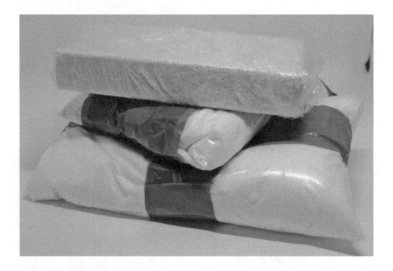

Picture of two 1-kilo packs of cut cocaine and a 1-kilo block of cocaine paste (courtesy of Martin Vickerman). The street purity of cocaine is anywhere from 5% to 40% depending on where the dealer is in the food chain of delivery. Cocaine is often cut (mixed with other substances) by a dealer who buys a quantity sufficient to able to cut the purity further to fund their own habit.

Cocaine paste is imported into the UK and found when you are close to the importation source. The purity of cocaine paste varies depending on the source of production. What are the purities of this street drug in your country?

A picture of a broken block of cocaine paste seized in a raid at the home of a UK dealer. The block has already started to be broken down and likely cut with any powder that is white and is a useful bulking agent for the cocaine paste. Cocaine is a stimulant drug.

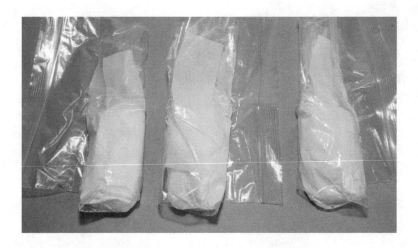

Pictures of bulk bags of amphetamine sulphate. Amphetamine in the UK is the most cut drug, with most purities being in the region of 6%. Amphetamine is a stimulant that is often cut with cocaine. As a drug on its own, habitual use can cause rapid weight loss and other symptoms.

Pictures of multiple packs of amphetamine bulk buys to be sold or broken down into smaller purchases.

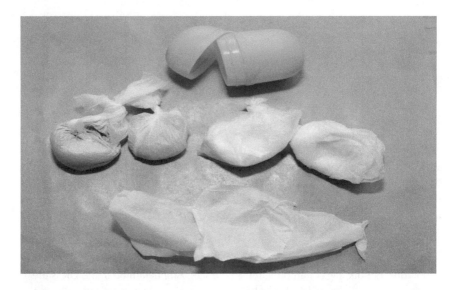

The confectionary toy container is used for the secretion of many drugs, including amphetamine.

Pictures of smaller packs (wraps) of amphetamine sulphate ready for distribution on the streets or into the workplace.

The pictures on this page show ecstasy tablets designed to look like hand-grenades or minions. Let's be clear: when people buy drugs that look like this they know what they are buying into, though the drugs may be fake or genuine. The fact is, prescribed medication manufacturers do not make tablets that look like cartoon characters or weapons. One ecstasy tablet can cause death. The user has no idea what underlying medical conditions can be activated by taking a drug that increases the heart rate or decreases the hydration levels of the body.

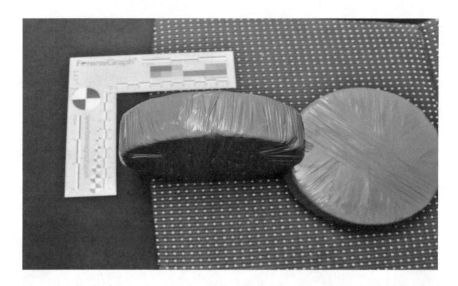

The two round cakes when opened were discovered to be heroin. The purity of heroin tends to have the same purity as cocaine. One problem with heroin is the current trend to cut it with fentanyl, which has caused a great many deaths. Heroin is probably the worst drug on which to have a dependency, although all drug dependency is dangerous.

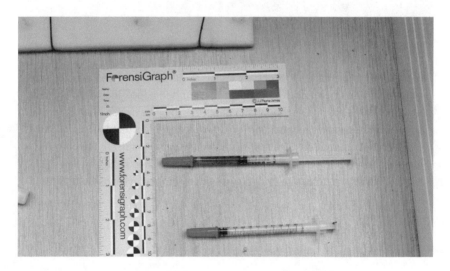

Pictures of syringes used and prepared for the injection of heroin.

Pictures of synthetic drugs as shown on the internet. Synthetic drugs were not regulated until the introduction of the Psychoactive Substances Act 2016. What is the situation in your country with regard to synthetic drugs designed to mimic the effects of illegal substances?

Prescribed medications in the workplace can be a major issue, especially strong painkillers and opiate-based drugs. The instant test devices for saliva and urine cannot detect heroin. They rely on detecting an opiate metabolite, which then requires the donor to be suspended and a back to laboratory sample submitted to identify the 6-monoacetylmorphine (6MAM) metabolite that is heroin. The control in the workplace of prescribed medications is the legally prescribed medication under the control of a GP (doctor). Many prescribed medications are controlled drugs within criminal legislations. What is the situation in your country? If the employee is in possession of a prescribed medication illegally then they are likely committing a criminal or civil offence. Have you adjusted your substance misuse policy to reflect this situation in your country? Many strong opiate painkillers allow an employee to attend work with debilitating symptoms, but are they in reality fit for work? Are they just rendered fit for attendance at work? Are they self-medicating with black market prescribed medications or stockpiled repeat prescription outside of the control of a GP or current prescription? You need to know.

Above is a picture of £6,000, the proceeds of drug dealing from some of the pictures in this section. The drug dealer's goal is rapid untaxed wealth. Drug dealing carries no quality control system or complaints procedure. Drug dealers do not care about what they are pushing or what it does to the end users, their families or work colleagues. They do not care about the lives and communities they are destroying. The employer is in an exceptional position to manage these problems in society that also manifest in the workplace. The employer has to comply with a wide range of criminal and civil legislations as well as country-specific statutory requirements. The workplace substance misuse programme helps the employer make the workplace a safe place to be and has the ability to influence a change in substance and alcohol misuse culture in their local communities, and as a collective, their nations. Governments need to support their industry leaders in this countermeasure. It's the most efficient way to manage substance and alcohol misuse in society.

Foreword

When I embarked on my training, at the start of my career some 25 years or so ago, I remember my senior lecturer telling me that I was to be a 'friend of the human race'. It was the motto (in Latin of course) of the professional association that I would join so that I could practise my skills, make a difference to those less fortunate and earn a living. It has taken me some considerable time to revisit how I may have achieved this. I am still trying to abide by that motto.

I have been fortunate; life hasn't caught me out and led me to become addicted to or misuse drugs or alcohol. I am a product of a generation that was told by the government to 'Just Say No'. And I did. But there is an inescapable truth we are all witness to: relaxation of drug laws, easier access to illegal substances, cheaper alcohol and normalization within our culture of the effects these have on people and society. We know this, and we see this on any street in any town, city or country we visit. We may even partake in it to a greater or lesser extent, because we can.

One of the first things clients say to me when I am helping them with accident investigations in the workplace is 'We have a policy for that.' Inevitably the policy is reviewed, and we will assess all elements of it and apply it to the process of undertaking a robust investigation, identifying causes and targeting improvement to preclude that specific accident from happening again. Over the last 5 years, people who are tasked with managing workplace safety systems interject this discussion with 'We drug test them and if they are positive for any alcohol or drugs then we will discipline them.' So, the penalty within the workplace is that you might get fired.

This has since manifested itself in workplace drugs and alcohol policies becoming normalized. Does this tell us that we generally accept that there is a risk that workers are working while under the influence of drugs? I believe we would all answer that with some acceptance. Therefore, there is a duty to identify it and act on it; otherwise, the safety laws we work within will be breached in a number of possible ways.

Most of us will have done it: we are entirely comfortable with having some painkillers, cold remedies and health supplements in our possession and taken before, during and after work, even while driving, where most of us are acutely aware that there is some law that makes drug-driving an offence. But those painkillers make driving possible, don't they? For some of us this can include injectable drugs used to manage conditions such as diabetes.

My growing interest in workplace drug and alcohol policies was elevated when I heard that there was this man I had to meet; he was making a difference in this very specific subject area. It had occurred to me that the general wording in the ubiquitous drugs and alcohol policy didn't really explain what 'positive for alcohol or drugs' really meant, but having a policy was better than not having one surely? I finally got to meet Trevor Hall and a quick meeting became an afternoon meeting, that became more phone calls, emails and sharing of best practice and reviewing these policies for a myriad of clients, attending seminars together and being given the honour of introducing him and his work to you in this foreword.

Trevor has an ability to apply, not only the law, but also the reality we are all living in, to his work. He will methodically look at what an employer is attempting to do and highlight how the policy will not deliver the controls or assurance that it was created for. He has a deep understanding of the entire substance misuse in the workplace field and unrivalled experience in determining what might be sufficiently robust to stand up to courtroom scrutiny, employment tribunal analysis and counsel's opinion.

But more importantly, at this moment in time, he has started to do something about it that will help our friends, colleagues, business leaders and workers.

I am very privileged to be able to work alongside Trevor Hall. In addition to his passion for this subject matter and his mission to make better not only the workplace, its people and the wider elements of society that substance misuse affects, he has also recognized what needs to change, how it can be changed and how it can genuinely be done to make a difference.

I look forward to seeing Trevor's work continue to make a difference. It has done so in businesses I have introduced him to, he is helping people manage the workplace around substance misuse and addictions. If you take the time to read what he says and engage with his advice he will undoubtedly be able to help you with your business. He is a friend of the human race – Trevor Hall Amicus Humani Generis.

Phillip Morton BSc(Hons) LLB(Hons) MCIEH
Principal Risk Consultant

Acknowledgements

- My business partner, Gordon Angus
- My good friend, Phillip Morton
- Matrix Diagnostics & Cansford Laboratories
- Professors Sheila McQueen & Jonathan Ling
- Routledge

Introduction

My first negative experience of substance misuse in the workplace was in 1967 when I joined the Royal Navy and caught a friend injecting heroin. I was, at the time, the class leader of 36 young 15-to 16-year-olds embarking on a 12-year naval career straight from school. When I saw the state my friend was in, having already injected, I experienced fear and trepidation about his welfare and his incoherent state of gouching out, which at that time I was unaware of and had not been trained to identify. As young naval ratings we had received some education around the topic of illegal drugs; it was after all, the age of flower power. What we were not trained for was what to do when it directly confronted you and what your responsibilities would be, not just as a junior leader but also as a friend. In reality I had no choice; as soon as I called a medic to his attention the whole situation was taken out of my hands, the naval discipline code kicked in, my friend was taken away to a military hospital and then to naval detention quarters. We never saw him again, as he was dishonourably dismissed the service. During that blur of rapid response, I was simply told I had done the right thing, though it didn't feel that way when I had to get in the boxing ring with the rest of my friends who felt I had done the wrong thing. I put the whole experience down to a learning curve in life when dealing with a friend's problem and the protection of life. Throughout the remainder of my naval service the biggest problem was the management of alcohol, bearing in mind that once you achieved the age of 21 you were entitled to a large tot (measure) of very strong 54% navy rum, every day. Add to this, from the age of 16 you were entitled to also draw down on 600 free cigarettes per month for the rest of your naval service. None of these approaches was conducive to the physical wellbeing of either your liver or lungs. I chose not to smoke and sold my ration of cigarettes to supplement the then low wages. Despite the best efforts of naval discipline, the black market in strong rum was abundant.

In 1979 I joined a UK police constabulary on completion of my 12 years in the military. This was a different experience, involving enforcement and application of a wide variety of laws from the late 1970s onward, many directed towards the protection of life and property and the prevention and detection of crime. These were the vague recollections of my oath to the crown of England taken in the presence of a magistrate. There was less thought given to the proactive consequences of drugs on the individual and more towards the detection of crimes relating to illegal drugs. Yes, I attended the post-mortems of drug deaths, whether by overdose or more violent situations such as fatal road traffic accidents and the occasional killings or suicides. The overriding process of substance misuse management here was, and depending on your view, either the effective or ineffective, application of the UK criminal justice system. In dealing with the living victims of substance misuse or fatalities I started to take a closer look at countermeasures in place and those not in existence, forming a different opinion of what could be done and very much looking at the impotence of the police and the criminal justice system's approach to managing the issue from casual use all the way through to large-scale drug dealing, importation and manufacturing massive amounts of drugs. Of course, there was a range of illegal substances in regular use, but in those days you were identified by your drug of choice, e.g. a dope head, a smack head, a coke head and so on. Cocktail substance misuse was not as prominent as it is today; the purity of drugs was not as good as it is today; and the quantity of drugs was not as abundant as it is today. The consequences of prosecution then were more significant than they are today. The tetrahydrocannabinol (THC) content in cannabis was nowhere near the levels we now find in modern hybrids of cannabis plants. Levels have moved from 4% THC to over 40% THC, and you cannot compare the two substances in the same context anymore. So, the circle is complete: within many situations, when an illegal activity is low in volume the penalties are high. Now that the illegal activity is high in volume the penalties are low, usually based on the fact there are not enough resources to cope with day-to-day management or enforcement of an issue that has a massive impact on individuals and society as a whole or sits outside of a range of newly perceived optional priorities.

Just short of 16 years in UK law enforcement and after many home office residential courses I became a victim of substance misuse myself when my daughter got herself into a huge amount of trouble with drugs while I was a serving as a drug squad officer, despite my best efforts as a parent and serving officer. At that time, she was 15 years of age and was the victim of rape by one of my own informants. She turned to drugs as a means of managing that situation and has continued to have major self-esteem issues. As a family we received no help from my then police employer or any of the social services; we were left to our own methods of dealing with each other while I was still serving as a very busy detective. In the end, we decided that as I had combined my navy and police pension the best course of action was to leave the police and relocate to our home town, some 250 miles away from that employment and those unresolved problems. It did not help the rehabilitation of my only child nor did it specifically help my marriage, which has now lasted 46 years despite these difficulties. My daughter is now 42 years of age and continues to cause my wife and myself immense concern and many sleepless nights over her poor judgement in the face of so much of her own dysfunction, mental health and pain to all of us. She is still, however, much loved and forever part of our family.

We now have three grandchildren and a great-grandchild on the way and despite being left to our own resolve in the management of our situation in those early days within the family environment, the despair and frustration that is a constant shadow over what we strive to do and achieve in life became a subject I wanted to deal with.

The realization during my daughter's early support through social services was that there was very little help for the innocent victims of someone else's dalliances into illegal drugs and their wider criminality, e.g. the family unit. While the users of drugs are seen as victims, there are a great many more who become victims of substance misuse through association with those who misuse illegal and legal substances, either as family members, friends, work colleagues or employers. Employers have the worst of it, as they have to consider legislations that can be applied to them by taking no action or the wrong action when substance misuse manifests itself in the workplace in many forms across every sector and every society's employment pool globally.

On leaving the police in 1994 I became a specialist corporate and commercial investigator working globally, investigating organized crime infiltration as well as the usual opportunist crimes of fraud, product diversion, theft, money laundering via anti-terrorist activity. I also investigated the enforcement of a variety of global criminal legislations. Brand protection was a major issue for many original equipment manufacturer (OEM) companies and there was also the ever-present drug use, trafficking, infiltration into global shipping routes, etc. What I found over the next 25 years to date was how unprepared the employer is in managing these criminal activities, especially substance misuse in the workplace. It also reinforced the lack of resources the police have in the management of many crimes that have no borders, and jurisdiction is always an issue where a force does not want to register an undetectable crime. I have repeatedly found in Eastern and Western Europe a worse situation where many police officers are not prepared to take certain risks where their pay is so low and the risk to their life is so high. What can be done to help them?

When I decided to write this book and the subsequent series of books, *Drugs & the Workplace: A Guide for...* Professions/Sectors, it was in the knowledge that there is very little constructive information that helps knowledge transfer on the subject either between sectors or across specific professions. Many legislations are applied to manage specific situations, but very little formal training is available that is effective, legally defensible or best understood by those charged with managing the subject and those who offend against those legislations in the workplace. I looked back at the home office courses I attended as a fledgling UK detective in the 1980s and came to the conclusion that they were not the best answer for the employer around substance misuse in the workplace or in society with regard to either the local employment pool or the delivery of corporate governance. It was clear to me that successive governments were wasting millions in taxpayers' money on trying to manage the minority as opposed to helping the employer manage the majority of the working population. In addition to that wasted millions of tax revenue there was the everlasting list of terms used to dilute the dangers of substance misuse, the most obvious being the term recreational drug use. Recreational use is not used with regard to car theft, assault or other criminal acts that can carry a lesser sentence on conviction than those of illegal substance misuse. Add to this, the paucity of the response of the criminal justice system, which together with successive governments has created a massive subculture, not a minority of individuals, who seek untaxed rapid wealth at any cost and without fear of the long-term consequences to society. The penal system for those incarcerated is not allowed to, or is ignoring, the use of substances in the prison system where staffing levels are stretched to the limits of effectiveness and with little or no rehabilitation of those who are incarcerated. There are simple and effective methods to solve these issues; some more draconian than others, but needs must. On release from custody ex-offenders are pushed into the workplace as part of their repatriation, or are they?

In the workplace the employer is battered with additional taxes, legislations and many of the responsibilities that are charged to those who manage society or those within the direct control of government and local authorities. What those governments and authorities have failed to grasp is that 35 million or more people in the UK and billions of adults in the global employment pool can be influenced by the way the employer can change a substance misuse culture and its correlation to criminality for the benefit of society. By bringing to bear the countermeasures and agencies that have limited success in managing society or by providing the support that cannot be found in overstretched public service sectors, the employer stands alone, bearing many funding responsibilities that should be supported by government and diverted from a range of dysfunctional support mechanisms. The same is true in many countries, although some governments are more proactive than others and some are more barbaric in response to the violent conditions the criminal elements impose on society by ignoring the rules of society. In my many and protracted travels all over the world, I have come to the conclusion that the best and most rational way of managing substance misuse in society is through the workplace and in due course the workplace helping society and educational establishments.

So, let's help the employer and let's support the employer with initiatives from the government. Let's take personal gain or kudos away from what every government knows should be done and how it should be done. Let's help the employer, help the employee, help society, help the generations to come. Some will say it is everyone's right to work; it's hard to argue against. It is, however, every employee's legal duty to be fit for work under a range of civil and criminal legislations, statutory requirements or terms and conditions (T&Cs) of employment, no matter where they live or work in the world. It is right that every potential employee and existing employee is managed with dignity and due process no matter what situation is being applied, no matter what consequence of what action is being applied. What I have found is that many substance misuse policies are drawn from the internet or have been compiled by people charged with the job but not qualified to deliver it. Too many companies see it as a tick in the box instead of a culpability under those legislations and statutory requirements. Too many policies are not reflective of the corporate governance that drives a company. Too many T&Cs of employment are lacking due to too little knowledge. I am a firm believer that certain situations can only have one outcome and that where criminal activity is frustrating or impacting negatively on the workplace then it needs to be eradicated through zero tolerance. Liberal attitudes to substance misuse do not have a part to play where safety, the law and moral duty are applied in return for wages. I hope this book will start to stimulate your thinking around what is a very complicated subject and a profession in its own right.

Dedication

I'm still married to Pamela today. She has stayed with me and witnessed and shared many of my experiences and frustrations that have evolved into the contents of this book and the others to follow. I dedicate this book to my wife and my family, who have been the victims of my passion in the protection of life and the detection or prevention of those issues that have a negative impact to the workplace globally, society globally and individuals globally.

1 | People, drugs and the workplace

Introduction

There is a need to build awareness concerning how drugs impact people and ultimately the workplace. This chapter is not designed to give the reader extensive training in substance misuse and the management of people caught up in it. Rather it is a basic look at some of the traditional thinking and reasons why people misuse substances and alcohol, as well as issues and considerations you may be faced with in the process of managing your workplace Substance and Alcohol Misuse Policy (SAMP), workplace Programme Of Testing (POT) and workplace Employee Assistance Programme (EAP). Most of all, it provides additional information for the employees themselves within an overall Substance Misuse Management Programme (SMMP).

More and more companies nationally and globally are engaging with workplace wellbeing initiatives that examine both the physical and mental health assessments of their workforce and of contractors who work with them. Workplace testing for drugs, alcohol and other substances (legal or otherwise) has been accepted for some time and indeed mandated in many circumstances, across many industries. In the UK, public sector and certain private sector industries mandate or are subject to mandatory testing in a variety of legislative and job-specific situations, most allied to physical/mental health wellbeing for those job-specific/sector-specific reasons, induction protocols and so on. Airline pilots and air traffic controllers are subject to much more stringent alcohol cut-off levels; the same is true of train conductors, rail trackside workers and other professions. Why would we not consider our insurance obligations and apply them to every UK employee's *fiduciary duty* to be *fit for work*? *What is the law in your country around the employee's legal duty to be fit for work?*

Most employers have a zero-tolerance policy with regard to illegal substance use; there is, however, a fragmented and under-reported approach to the impact of legally prescribed medications in the workplace, especially the use and misuse of opiates.

All aspects of workplace activity depend on the employee's engagement with the company's business philosophy, governance and business activities, at and away from the workplace while on duty. It has been my approach, as mentioned previously, that any UK workplace substance and alcohol misuse programme emanates from UK law, which requires that

'It is an employee's *Fiduciary Duty* to be *Fit for Work*'

How do you manage that duty or even examine/measure that fitness at any given moment in the UK or in your own country? How do you identify what constitutes culpabilities in law? What are the responsibilities applied to a job description/terms and conditions (T&Cs) of employment? Now that Canada has legalized the personal use and possession of cannabis, how is that country going to examine/measure an employee's fitness for work? Fitness to drive? Fitness to be in charge of a child? And there is much more. In addition, how will that country manage the combined use/misuse of cannabis with other legal or illegal substances?

The employer will always have a more profitable business when the workplace is harmonious, productive and above all a safe place to be. There is no doubt that the use of illegal substances and some misuse of legal substances are a disruptive element in the workplace that leads to loss, intimidation, an unpleasant employee environment and preventable mental and physical health issues (see Chapter 6 on workplace culture mapping). There has been a steady evolution of some sectors into a working environment that has stretched the meaning of the term 'employee engagement' within the workplace. The erosion of some full-time employment positions and a truly living wage is due in part to issues such as:

- Zero hours contracts
- More reliance on lower paid agency staff than on full-time staff
- Seasonal work/temporary contracts, etc.
- The peaks and troughs of the economy, whether national or global
- In the service industry, the employee's reliance on tips to enhance low pay, and so on

While employees in these situations may feel disengaged there is a huge requirement for the employer to engage with a range of circumstances under the threat of prosecution, fines or operational mechanisms and business development/monitoring in areas such as:

- Health & safety legislation
- Employment law
- Insurance cover and risk assessment
- Statutory requirements
- Environmental compliance issues
- Public liability insurance
- Professional indemnity insurance
- A variety of other indemnity insurances
- A plethora of civil and criminal litigations, constantly changing
- Risk-averse banking and funding options that cause shortcuts or restrict investment
- Working time directives (EU)
- Industry-specific accreditations
- Personnel development
- Immigration legislations
- Maternity/paternity leave
- Mandatory pension planning for staff, and so much more

The list goes on. At what point does the employee engage with the employer who is already compelled to engage with a great many compulsory obligations/regulations, including civil and criminal legislations combined with statutory requirements, many of which are missing from T&Cs of employment? An employer wants to become an employer of choice and attract a higher calibre of employee into a safe working environment. An employee wants to have a safe working environment free of fear of intimidation, which is supportive and inclusive to all, especially with a wage that makes it possible for employees and their families to live reasonably comfortable and stress-free lives.

This chapter is further designed in terms of awareness of both parties' obligations and commitment, specifically in the area of substance and alcohol misuse in the workplace. There is a direct correlation between illegal drug use and criminality, purely by the manner in which illegal substances are bought/sold, manufactured and legislated against, anywhere in the world. Many companies and people are unaware that the misuse of prescribed medications is also a major issue, not just for the workplace but also across society, especially opiate misuse/dependency. If the media is to be believed, substance misuse is an epidemic within the global society. *The workplace must manage issues that are not being best managed in society, for a variety of reasons.* This is evidenced by a great many UK and other nations' law enforcement agencies stating they will not attend to or even deal with low-level drug misuse, a stark contrast to the situation in the Philippines.

The problem lies in the fact that drugs are an escalation product; a user will very rarely stay at the level of use right from the start and then all the way through the journey of misuse/abuse. A drug will become less effective, the body will become more tolerant and before long things will have escalated out of control and what was a low-level misuse has become a mental or physical wellbeing issue, dependency or a problem across multiple issues, some of which are outlined near the end of this chapter.

The new drug driving regulations announced in England, Wales and Northern Ireland in March 2015 now set a different standard of compliance and include a wider variety of offences that can be committed by a company, its management structure and employees collectively. *What are the drink/drug driving regulations that apply in your country? What offences can be committed by the employee and the employer around your legislations? How do you mitigate against them in your policy? How do you apply them to an employee's T&Cs of employment?*

Example

Two UK subcontract employees travel to a principal contractor's road construction operation some 200 miles from their depot. On arrival they are required to go through an induction protocol with the principal contractor, which includes a substance and alcohol test. At this point both decline the induction, as they have smoked cannabis on the way to the contract site in their 30-tonne truck. They contact their manager to explain why they cannot fulfil the contractual requirement, at which point their manager tells them to drive the vehicle back to the depot and he will see them in the morning for a disciplinary investigation.

What that manager has done is to tell his staff to drive a heavy goods vehicle (truck) on a road under the influence of cannabis. Had the crew been stopped on the return journey and tested, routinely or post-accident, that manager could have been charged with an aiding and abetting, counselling or procuring a drug driving offence in the UK. That manager could have been found guilty of the same offence as the driver; in the event there had been a fatality the consequences would have been very substantial for all concerned. The company insurance provisions will be challenged and again mitigated for future premiums or even had the existing insurance premium negated.

More recent UK legislation with regard to the Insurance Act 2015 came into force on 12 August 2016. The act requires that the insurance industry conduct a full risk assessment of their clients' operations so that adequate insurance can be legally provided or mitigated for; in my opinion this should include the client's substance and alcohol misuse countermeasures or lack thereof. *What are the insurance regulations in your country? How do you mitigate them in your substance and alcohol misuse countermeasures and other policies?*

The new insurance act also requires that the insured party makes fair presentation of the company's risk exposure to the insurer so that they can comply with the act. *What are your duties in your country when applying for insurance within your business operations? How do you mitigate them against business operations and a coherent raft of polices to identify what constitutes a breach of that policy? Is your policy robust enough to protect the business and those who work in it?*

What impact has this new insurance act had on the workplace?

Workplace insurance premiums are rising when they should be falling, especially where so many legislations, old and new, are now being applied to company owners and managers. Since the UK act came into force in 2016 there has been a significant increase in the denials of workplace insurance claims, mostly around the fact the company had not made fair presentation to its insurer for insurance protection.

If you think substance and alcohol misuse is not a risk in your workplace you will find out at your expense when things go wrong and you have not made fair presentation or taken appropriate steps. When so many government agencies and healthcare providers are stating substance misuse in all forms is so bad in society, why do we ignore it in the workplace? What is the situation in your country?

New UK/European General Data Protection Regulation (GDPR) has a set standard that raises the bar with regard to other key areas of managing and exposing personal data. With respect to workplace substance and alcohol misuse policy writing and programme building around testing and employee assistance, it has increased the level of scrutiny on employers with regard to:

- How permissions are obtained for the testing of employees
- What instructions were given and recorded with regard to an employee's knowledge of any signed consent
- Understanding that consent cannot be assumed because it is written into policy and the need for it to be explained and signed for when understood
- The documentation required across those areas of consent
- How training is conducted and recorded
- How testing is conducted and applied within T&Cs of employment
- How the employer/analytical services apply the keeping and processing of the details of donors' samples for positives and negative results
- The requirement of analytical laboratories to comply within their own accreditations such as UKAS 1705, FDA and so on

'Beware of the hidden threat posed by substance and alcohol mis-use in the workplace and its correlation to criminality. Beware of not responding properly to programmes of information management within and outside of your control.'

– Trevor Hall

What are the personal data management protocols in your country? How do you apply them to your policy writing, programme building and implementation? What are the consequences of getting it wrong?

Company directors and senior as well as junior managers/supervisors must be aware, more than ever, of the criminal offences of Aid, Abet, Counsel or Procure. In the UK, for these to be considered indictable and summary offences in criminal cases, proof beyond all reasonable doubt is required. The terms can also be applied when looking for culpability/responsibility in civil litigation.

Remember these are definitions in UK law. *What is the law in your country?*:

Beyond all reasonable doubt: Magistrate/Crown Court
Balance of probability: Tribunal/Civil Court

What are the burdens of proof within your country's criminal justice system as well as civil legislations that have an impact on your culpability or responsibility?

UK definitions of Aid, Abet, Counsel or Procure

- **'To Aid'** is to give help, support or assistance and it will generally, although not necessarily, take place at the scene of the crime/offence. It is not necessary to prove that there was any agreement between the principal and the alleged accessory, nor is there a need to prove a causative link between the aid and the commission of the offence by the principal.
- **'To Abet'** is to incite, instigate or encourage and this can be committed only by an accessory who is present when the crime/offence is committed. This does imply either an express or implied agreement between the parties although there is no need to prove any causative link between what the abettor did and the commission of the offence.
- **'To Counsel'** is to encourage and most usually covers advice, information, encouragement or the supply of equipment before the commission of a crime/offence. It implies agreement with the principal.
- **'To Procure'** means to produce by endeavour, by setting out to see that it happens and taking the appropriate steps to produce that happening. The principal can be entirely 'innocent' of the procurer's acts so long as there is proof of a causal link between the procuring and the commission of the offence by the principal offender, e.g., as in *AG's Reference (No 1) (1975)* 2 AER 684, spiking a drink procures a drunk-driving offence.

Under the Magistrates Court Act a person who aids, abets, counsels or procures the commission by another person of a summary offence shall be guilty of the like offence.

This has become a major consideration not just in the writing of a policy in the UK but also in the way managers and company directors are guided or trained. What is the impact in your country?

The impairment discussion

Avoid building your Substance and Alcohol Misuse Policy (SAMP) around the definition of impairment, as this is a judgemental issue that is confused by the lack of education of staff or expert evidence testimony applied at the time a judgement is made. It is further confused across the side effects of legal and illegal substances and the signs or symptoms of a great many ailments brought into the workplace by the workforce. See Chapter 3 on the writing, development and implementation of a workplace SAMP. Appearing impaired is a different argument and can take many forms; the smell of intoxicating liquor is one of many. Impairment because a positive result is provided in not good enough; this is where the SAMP must be applied and embedded into strict T&Cs of employment, supported by a statutory requirement (limiting use of certain medications to specific levels). Impairments can be visible or not obvious or immediately apparent.

What are the statutory requirements in your country with regard to driving while taking prescribed intravenous methadone? Or with regard to a regular chronic misuse/abuse of illegal and legal substances?

The impaired cognitive abilities and shortcomings in judgement of an employee who is under the influence of one or more substances is a major concern to the health & safety of that employee and his or her colleagues, as well as the business in which they work. In the UK, across most workplace situations, T&Cs of employment and other policies should revolve around the fact it is an employee's *Fiduciary Duty* to be fit for work. Any self-inflicted situation in which the employee is not fit for work or in compliance within a range of policies generally allows the company to invoke its disciplinary procedure, depending on the severity of the situation, up to and including dismissal.

The following is a small selection of UK acts for you to consider. *Can you list similar acts and sections that will have a bearing on your workforce and the policies you will need to put in place?* Do not put acts and sections into policy! It is enough to state a range of applicable civil and criminal legislations, as there are so many acts and legislations available for application it would not be possible to name or defend them all to the letter of the law, and of course legislation changes over time. There are numerous other legislations that may also have an impact on your business and your approach to substance and alcohol misuse management strategies and policy development, as outlined in Chapter 3.

Most countries will have a similar set of legislations that can be brought to bear in the development of the company's SAMP, POT and EAP. These and other situations need to be considerations in T&Cs of employment, training, consent and so on.

In the UK we have many civil and criminal legislations that can be applied to the workplace, a few of which are outlined in the following text. *What are they in your country/sector-specific situations?*

The Misuse of Drugs Act 1971

S. 5. (1) States that it shall not be lawful for a person to have a controlled drug in his/her possession except under certain circumstances. This act also covers activities relating to, producing, supplying, preparing or using controlled drugs.

S.8. Provides that it an offence for a person, if being the occupier or concerned in the management of *any* premises, to knowingly permit or suffer any of the following activities to take place on those premises:
(a) Unlawfully producing or attempting to produce a controlled drug
(b) Unlawfully supplying or attempting to supply a controlled drug to another, or offering to supply a controlled drug to another
(c) Preparing opium for smoking
(d) Smoking cannabis, cannabis resin or opium

S. 21 States: *Where any offence under [the] Act committed by a body corporate is proved to have been committed with the consent of, or connivance of or to be attributed to any neglect on the part of any director, manager, secretary or other similar officer of the body corporate or any person purporting to act in any such capacity, he/she as well as the body corporate shall be guilty of that offence & shall be liable to be proceeded against.*

Drugs Act 2005

Increases the power of the police and the courts in relation to drug control. The police can test drug offenders on arrest, which will require those testing positive to undergo or be referred for treatment. It also empowers the police to authorize or conduct intimate searches or use X-ray or ultrasound scans on people suspected of having concealed Class A drugs with the intention to supply, import or export them.

Corporate Manslaughter Act 2006

S.1. (1) States: *any organisation to which this act applies is guilty of an offence if the way in which its activities are managed or organised:*
(a) *Causes a person's death.*
(b) *Amounts to a gross breach of a relevant* duty of care *owed by the organisation to the deceased.*

Human Rights Act 1998

The *aims of the act* are to ensure that the rights of an individual as well as those of the community are protected. This means the rights of the individual may have to be balanced against those of another.

Article 8 states it's an individual's right to a private life and family. A Substance Misuse Policy is justified where public safety is at stake.

The act makes allowances for interferences where the aim is the protection of the health of others through existing legislations.

Management of the Safety at Work Regulations 1999

Regulation 3 of the act requires that a *'suitable & sufficient'* risk assessment be undertaken by employers to identify those at risk from company operations. This includes the requirement to assess the possible risks created by employees/contractors and visitors who may have taken controlled drugs or alcohol.

Health and Safety at Work Act 1974

S.2. (3) Dictates that all companies or organizations who employ more than five persons are to have a written statement of general health & safety policy.

S.2. (1) It is the general duty of both established and temporary employers to ensure as far as practicable the health & safety and welfare of all employees.

S.2. (2) (c) The employer has to provide *'such information, instruction, training and supervision as far is reasonably practicable for the health and safety at work of all employees'*.

S.7. (a) It is the duty of every employee *'to take reasonable care for the H&S of him/herself and other persons who may be affected by his/her acts or omissions at work'*.

S.7. (b) There is a duty on the part of every employee to co-operate with his or her employer *'so far as is necessary to enable that duty or requirement to be performed or complied with'*.

The Psychoactive Substances Act 2016

S.1. *In this act 'psychoactive substance' means any substance which:*
(a) *Is capable of producing a psychoactive effect in a person who consumes it*
and
(b) *Is not an exempted substance.*

There is no offence of possession or use of some of the substances under the Psychoactive Substances Act. Impairment and self-inflicted absence are issues for employers to manage within the policy. As of January 2017, K2 Spice and other synthetic cannabinoids are now controlled substances as Class B drugs under the Misuse of Drugs Act (MDA) and all offences of possession, use, trafficking and manufacturing of a Class B drug apply. The same is true of mephedrone, another Class B drug.

Insurance Act 2015

The upgrade to the Insurance Act 2015 has been applied in the UK as of 12 August 2016. It places greater emphasis on the insured to give a fair presentation of their business to insurers by:

- Disclosing all material circumstances via a reasonable search of the company.
- Including senior staff where necessary, especially if the person dealing with the insurances does not know this information.

To give a fair presentation now requires the client to give a fuller disclosure, and failure to disclose this to insurers, whether deliberate or not, can have the following consequences:

- A policy may be cancelled.
- Premiums paid may not be returned.
- If the misrepresentation is non-deliberate the options are proportionate and insurers can:
    (a) Decline your risk but must return the premiums paid
    or
    (b) Insurers can apply new terms, in light of the new information.

It is the opinion of Hall and Angus that substance and alcohol misuse in the workplace, including while on duty away from the workplace, is part of a full disclosure to their insurer to ensure the safety of the business, its employees and where appropriate contractors, visitors and the public.

Road Traffic Act 1988

The act states that it is an offence to drive or attempt to drive a motor vehicle while being unfit through drink or drugs. A further offence is committed whereby any person causes, aids or abets, counsels or procures such an offence.

The Drug Driving Regulations 2015

The new drug driving regulations now create an issue for employers in that they are liable for aid, abet, counsel or procure offences by allowing or causing employees to drive while unfit or impaired by both prescribed and illegal substances, as well as alcohol.

It is the duty of a GP or pharmacist to advise patients of any side effects of medications they prescribe or dispense that may impair the user's ability to drive or operate machinery or that render the user *Unfit for Work*. It is the duty of the person taking the medication to declare themselves unfit to drive or work machinery if the prescribed medication they are taking negatively impacts them or the compliance with their *Fiduciary Duty* to be fit for work.

> *Note: It is the duty of the manufacturers of medications to highlight for the drug driving situation the side effects of certain medications on the box or in the instructions contained within the box.*

Data Protection Act 1998 (GDPR 25/5/18)

Confidential records must be retained to demonstrate that the company has taken all reasonable and practicable precautions to safeguard the health & safety and welfare of its employees. These also include details of training and awareness seminars provided to employees and it is the intention of the company to hold results of drug and alcohol testing on personnel files. GDPR applies updated processes for handling of a person's information/details.

The Transport and Works Act 1992

This act makes it illegal for railway employees (including conductors, signallers and trackside engineers) to work if they under the influence of drugs or alcohol.

It also makes it a criminal offence for certain workers to be unfit through use of drugs and alcohol while working on railways, tramways and other guided transport systems. The operators of the transport system would also be guilty of an offence unless they had *shown all due diligence* in trying to prevent the commission of such an offence.

The Railway and Transport Safety Act 2003

This act extends the above legislation to include maritime and airline workers.

UK drink and drug driving limits and penalties

The current drug driving legislation in England and Wales has evolved as new illict and prescribed drugs have come to the market; I have no doubt that the list of new substances will grow as the years go by. It is extremely important that employers and their management teams are fully aware of what is illegal so that they do not unwittingly 'Aid, Abet, Counsel or Procure' an offence committed by any employee while on company business.

Never insert acts or sections of acts in a substance and alcohol misuse policy/programme. The ones you leave out will be equally as applicable as the ones you put in. The ones you put in will have to be defended in their entirety at litigation and will likely include all surrounding case laws. The preceding selection lists just a few of the many that can be applied. See Chapter 3 for further guidance.

> *Note: Scotland is not part of the UK drug driving regulations at this time. Also the legal drink driving limit in Scotland is lower than in the rest of the UK (see Chapter 3).*

Prescription medicines

1. It is illegal in England, Wales and Northern Ireland to drive with legal drugs in your blood if it impairs your driving.
2. It's an offence to drive if you have more than the specified limits of certain drugs in your blood and you haven't been prescribed them.

Employees should be advised to talk with their GP or pharmacist about prescribed or over-the-counter (OTC) medications that may impair their judgement, general mental and physical wellbeing or fitness for work. *What are the regulations in your country on this subject?*

At Hall & Angus we have started conducting a controlled study around the impact of prescribed medications in the workplace, especially codeine. The study will reflect the existing analytical processes for certain drugs using the test mediums of hair (head and body), fingernail clippings, saliva and urine. Early findings indicate an increase in the prescribing and repeat prescribing of some very debilitating drugs for protracted periods, with many users being prescribed the maximum dosage from the very start of the prescribing regime and subsequently being left using those high dosages far beyond the manufacturers' guidelines.

We have already discovered that the cut-off for legally prescribed codeine is inappropriate. The cut-off for codeine in saliva is set at 15 ng/ml. I have personally been taking a prescribed dosage of codeine and my results were 153 ng/ml for the 3 days I was legally allowed to take the maximum dosage. I continue to be prescribed codeine for pain management and while taking 90 milligrams of codeine in every 24 hours my results using saliva are being returned at 153 ng/ml, way above a toxicology cut off. In addition, 6 hours after taking my first two 30-milligram tablets of codeine I tested presumptive positive on an instant saliva device. The presumptive positives continue to be produced on the instant saliva devices and the back to laboratory (BTL) test results continue to be far above the 15 ng/ml cut-off applied in workplace disciplinary procedures. It is clear to me that the cut-offs for workplace testing of legally prescribed medications are not fit for purpose in the UK and likely also across the rest of the world. That study will continue and its findings reported across a wider population of users/medications in due course.

Some drugs are short-, medium- and long-term acting. Some are required to be increased over time, depending on how the prescribed drug responds with a person's physical or mental capacity to take the medication or continue with the treatment. A great many are powerful drugs that for obvious reasons require time for the user's body to adjust/respond and so on.

The biggest problem for the employer is to establish a structured mechanism to measure the employee's fitness for work and if necessary determine what reasonable adjustments can be made. It is also necessary to properly establish whether the employee is not fit for continued employment in his or her existing job role or with company (see Chapter 4 on EAP). For the employee, the situation is worse for the following reasons:

• Many employees, and company owners, take medications to be fit for work.
• A great many medications render the user unfit for work.
• A great many employees work in companies that have no structure to manage such situations.
• Employees often have to look after family members who have been prescribed debilitating drugs and so on.

A number of other areas are developing around the use/misuse of prescribed medications that will come from the Hall & Angus study. The most worrying aspect to date is the uncontrolled development of the black market for prescribed medications being sold to vast swathes of the population off prescription, many of which are used as bulking/cutting agents for other illegal substances or for use with alcohol. In addition, there is a need to investigate the prescribing regimes of GPs which may often be in contradiction of drug manufacturers' guidelines. *Do you have similar issues to be investigated in your country?*

Why you need a company substance and alcohol misuse policy

If the foregoing reasons have not convinced you of the need to have a proactive and reactive substance and alcohol misuse programme/mitigation in the management of the workplace, the workforce and the myriad illegal and legal substances being used, you may also want to consider the following issues that have also been identified in other studies:

• The negative on-cost of employing a substance misuser/abuser is quantifiable.
• The majority of substance misusers/abusers are in employment.

- Many employed misusers will sell or give illegal and legal drugs to work colleagues.
- Millions of work-days are lost per year.
- Higher rate of involuntary turnover of substance misusers/abusers in the workplace.
- Higher rate of absenteeism when comparing non-substance misusers/abusers to those who do not misuse/abuse.
- Higher agency and overtime costs are incurred to cover absenteeism.
- Higher rate of accidents and compensation claims with regard to substance misusers/abusers.
- Lower productivity and quality of end product associated with substance misusers/abusers.
- Uncontrolled workplace substance misuse is associated with a higher rate of criminality and intimidation in the workplace.
- Workplace intimidation has been shown to extend to local communities in off-site bullying and intimidation.
- Substance misusers/abusers have had multiple employers and failed workplace induction protocols in a short period of time.
- Substance misusers/abusers impose other on-costs for higher retraining and rehabilitation.
- Substance misusers/abusers incur higher micro-management costs and so on.

Case studies have shown that the demographic substance misuse/abuse cultures of the employment pool also transfer to the workplace. Local community activities do influence the nature and culture of the workforce and vice versa; see Chapter 6 on the Hall & Angus workplace culture map. Depending on the product of the business/service there is a natural black market for stolen raw materials or diverted product to fuel demographic cultures of organized and opportunist crime; see Chapter 7 on workplace investigations. The employment pool for industry and commerce varies but once again demographic influences may dictate the response of the pre-employment and recruitment strategies of a company (local knowledge).

Example

A global manufacturer of domestic goods also manufactured at a UK site. The UK site employed a high percentage of agency staff. The high turnover of management had diluted operational accountability, as did the outsourcing of accounts and compliance issues to other parts of the company or a totally outsourced provider. The breakdown in workplace continuity between departments and lack of controls for discrepancy/reconciliation reporting allied to poor perpetual inventory practices allowed the facility to descend into the control of those involved in organized and opportunist local crime, including drug dealing and widespread substance misuse in the local community and workplace. Through a mixture of pure theft, collusion between staff and organized crime and product diversion the facility was losing raw materials as well as significant quantities of finished product. The local demographics for drug abuse reflected high levels of cocaine, cannabis and heroin dependency.

Losses to the business were unsustainable, with the following results:

1. Off-shore company headquarters took a commercial decision to rationalize the facility and move most of the production out of the UK and into other European countries.
2. Information that impacted the preceding decision was discovered by placing an undercover employee into the workforce and by an independent risk assessment of loss against production, etc.
3. As a result, the site was reduced in size by around 75% with the subsequent manufacturing buildings and land being sold for housing. A larger fiscal loss was sustained by local communities and businesses.

Example

A large retail operation had lost control of its distribution centre (DC) to organized and opportunist crime. Again, a large proportion of the workforce was agency (80%), mostly because of complications around employee TUPE (Transfer of Undertakings Protection of Employment) law in the UK. Key staff positions that would usually be held by fully skilled and full-time employees were outsourced or given to agency staff not best suited or trained for the position, and not paid adequately for the responsibility. As a result of workplace intimidation and blackmail related to drug misuse/dealing on site, criminals gained the upper hand with regard to the issuance of forklift licences and were subsequently able to control stock locations for theft. In addition, insufficient oversight was placed on staff who were tasked with controlling computer systems for the goods receiving/picking and relocation of stock on site and via an e-commerce operation.

Stock controls onto delivery vehicles to retail outlets nationally were inappropriate, as were the practices for goods received at the retail outlets. A good many other issues clouded the full picture. Despite staff entering and leaving the DC via a range of security protocols, these were overridden by an outsourced security operation with an insufficient and ineffective Service Level

23

Agreement (SLA) and Key Performance Indicator (KPI) controls. This allowed for mass theft of high-value stock with no structured countermeasures or discrepancy/reconciliation reporting in place. As a result:

1. The UK company faced problems head on and introduced most of the recommendations of an independent risk assessment.
2. The company recovered control of all operations and removed temporary staff from key positions.
3. The company implemented further controls for electronic countermeasures and a workplace substance misuse programme.
4. More full-time staff were recruited and leadership training provided.
5. Outsourced security provider controls were revisited, modified and applied with strict SLAs and quantifiable KPIs.
6. As a result, the DC is operational with shrinkage and incidents reduced to within identified and controlled tolerance.
7. The company continues to trade profitably.

Example conclusions

- Commerce, industry and the community are the impact areas of the hidden, and often overt, threat of substance misuse and its correlation with criminality. In the workplace the threat posed by substance misuse is no less impactful than it is in the community, and the two are often inextricably linked.
- The approach to substance and alcohol misuse/abuse issues by commerce and industry can protect the business and the community where other strategies have already failed or are failing.
- With the employer, Hall & Angus is able to quantify the SAMP, POT and EAP programme effectiveness against a workplace return on investment (WROI) and measure its impact on the social return on investment (SROI). Our goal is to work with the insurance industry to mitigate these risks and impacts to commerce and industry.
- Companies must have a legal and structured means to deal with employees who feel the need to self-refer substance and alcohol misuse, including other issues that include use and misuse of prescribed medications.
- The cost of employing a substance/alcohol misuser/abuser as opposed to a non- misuser/abuser is quantifiable and has a significant financial

impact on the company in thousands of pounds or relevant currency, per employee, per year.

- Company strategy should therefore be to stop substance and alcohol misusers/abusers entering the workforce in the first instance while complying with a range of civil and criminal legislations, as well as country or sector specific statutory requirements.
- More also needs to be done to help those individuals who are excluded from work, due to substance and alcohol misuse abuse issues, to get back to work and become contributing members of society.
- Hall & Angus's activities and services show that it is possible to control and manage/educate out substance and alcohol misuse issues that have already negatively impacted the workplace or the individual.
- Studies prove the need for a range of substance and alcohol misuse/abuse testing methodologies allied to a range of investigative and rehabilitation methodologies.

So far, two specific phrases have been used:

1. *Substance Misuse*
2. *Substance Abuse*

A guide/opinion:

Misuse is considered for the purpose of this book as an occasional misuse, either voluntary or involuntary. *I do not recognize the term recreational substance misuse at all, either as a former drug squad detective or as a commercial investigator. Recreational use of illegal substances is a phrase coined by those who feel the need to justify its use outside of the law or the best interests of society. Illegal drug use is exactly that, ILLEGAL.*

Abuse has other connotations and is generally applied to those who are losing control or have lost control of their misuse and are moving toward or have become substance or alcohol dependent or have used one drug as a gateway to other drugs and to the culture of concealing it from everyone.

Let's build an awareness of how that *Misuse* and *Abuse* manifests in society and ultimately in the workplace. A formula has been used in certain circles called drug by type, set and setting. For the purpose of this book and acceptance into workplace terminology/understanding and guidance I have changed it to

25

Drug by Type – Individual Using – Location Used

Drug misuse/abuse comes in many forms and includes the misuse/abuse of legal and illegal substances. As stated earlier, the term 'recreational' when applied to illegal substances is a misnomer, as illegal substance misuse is criminal whichever way one looks at it and is not excusable.

- Do we say someone is a recreational car thief because they steal a car only when they need one or just for fun?
- Do we say someone is a recreational burglar because they burgle only at weekends and then only commercial premises?
- Do we say someone is a recreational criminal because they commit a crime in order to live?
- Do we say someone is a recreational drug dealer?

The penalties for a large proportion of car theft and burglary offences are lower than for some drug-related offences. Why the different attitude to drug-related issues and the lack of commitment to managing them out of the work-place and society?

With regard to cannabis, UK and global attitudes seem confused. In the 1960s, cannabis bush was around 5–7% pure in tetrahydrocannabinol (THC). Now there are a range of cannabis *hybrids* that can be grown in the UK and abroad which are more than 40% pure in THC. There is no comparison or argument between the two that allows them to be considered the same substance or, similarly to alcohol, set at controlled limits significantly below 40% pure cannabis. The hallucinogenic effects of modern cannabis and the resultant reported increased risk of developing schizophrenia have escalated *significantly* since the 1960s, rendering its use much more serious than 'recreational'.

So, in modern society some of the dangers of drug use depend on the

'Drug by Type' – 'Individual Using' – 'Location Used'.

- The *'Drug by Type'* is everything about the drug, how it is used, how often it is used, purity of the drug, reaction with or being mixed with other substances/cutting/bulking agents/alcohol and more.
- The *'Individual Using'* is everything connected with the person who is using the drug(s), their misuse/dependency, peer pressure, their own mental and physical health, vulnerability and more.

- The 'Location Used' is about where the person(s) use the drug(s), sub-stance, alcohol, etc., the dangers of the environment in which they are using, limitations in rapid emergency response and more.

To be clear, although the dangers of substance misuse are generally the result of these three issues either individually or collectively, there are other dangers to be taken into consideration, such as:

- Drugs being used to facilitate a crime, e.g., male and female rape.
- Drugs being used to groom people into the sex or human trafficking industry.
- Drugs being used to create a market that would not normally exist, such as a strong drug pushed into the market cheaply to increase dependency and then subsequently reduced in strength and increased in price to drive rapid untaxed wealth of criminal activity.
- Drugs used in gang initiations and other ceremonies.

The list goes on and becomes ever more ingenious as the types of drugs expand into any demographic.

Whereas alcohol levels can be tested using a single device the same cannot be said for drugs, and the analytical methods are not the same for testing all drugs. Different drugs have different dangers associated with them.

Drugs and other substances are more difficult to measure because of the life or even half-life of the drug metabolite and any cross-reactive compounds being looked for, *all being introduced into the body in different ways*. During the analytical process each individual drug or drug group responds only to an appropriate assay/reagent developed for the individual metabolite or cross-reactive compound. A variety or cocktail of drug metabolites along with their dubious cutting agents ingested by the human body can be eminently more dangerous than a variety/volume of alcoholic drinks, which are still danger-ous, but more so when all are taken simultaneously.

Some drugs, such as alcohol, heroin and tranquillizers, have a *sedative or depressant* effect which slows down the way the body and brain function. They can have a numbing effect that produces drowsiness if large quantities are consumed.

The accumulation of alcohol in the human body and the body's ability to eliminate it depends on a wide variety of factors. The one overriding factor is that time is the main antidote to alcohol being removed completely from the body, and other measures tend to ease the symptoms of a hangover.

- What is the impact on your business of employees being under the influence of or affected by the misuse of sedative or depressant drugs?
- What contingency planning do you have in place when misuse is discovered, self-assessed or self-referred?

Other drugs such as amphetamine, cocaine, crack and ecstasy have a *stimulant* effect, producing a rush of energy and increasing alertness. The foregoing questions apply to misuse of these drugs as well.

These two drug groups, depressants and stimulants, are often used together for a yin and yang effect.

Another group of drugs such as LSD, 'magic' mushrooms and to a lesser extent cannabis have *hallucinogenic* effects. This means they tend to alter the way the user feels, sees, hears, tastes or smells; see earlier for the same mitigation questions. The paragraphs that follow provide an overview for your information and consideration, with more detailed information available in clinical and medical reference books.

Depressants

Depressant drugs, such as too much alcohol and too much of or a very pure heroin can lead to a fatal overdose if a large quantity is consumed and especially if mixed. They can also affect co-ordination, cognitive abilities and judgement, making accidents more likely. Use of some depressant drugs may also lead to physical dependence and withdrawal symptoms with a serious impact on mental and physical wellbeing. The cutting agents used in depressant drugs are very often more potent than the drug itself; a single dose of a cutting agent such as fentanyl or car-fentanyl can be fatal on its own.

Stimulants

Drugs that speed up the central nervous system can produce anxiety or panic attacks, particularly if taken in large quantities. They can also be particularly dangerous for people who have heart or blood pressure problems. Stimulants can make people attempt activities beyond their physical capability, which can lead to injury to themselves or others. Many cutting agents for stimulants are themselves stimulants, such as amphetamine cut with cocaine.

Hallucinogens

Hallucinogenic drugs produce very disturbing experiences and may lead to erratic or dangerous behaviour by the user, especially if the individual is already unstable or having a 'bad trip'. The altered reality is not something you want to experience in any environment as it can lead to harm to self as well as others.

Painkillers

Painkillers, especially opiates, have become a major concern in the UK, leading to increasing numbers of people in the UK and globally developing opiate dependency. In North America and Canada the problem is much more severe. Generally, painkillers, both prescription and OTC, are readily misused and abused. There is a growing availability of opiate-based drugs on the dark web that enables those who have a dependency to go to multiple online doctors who offer prescriptions without cross reference to a patient's medical records. Strong painkillers such as fentanyl and car-fentanyl are used as cutting agents for other drugs, and as mentioned previously, a single use can be fatal.

New psychoactive substances

New psychoactive substances (NPS), known as 'legal highs', bath salts, spices and designer drugs, are manufactured to mimic the effects of other drugs. There is some evidence to suggest that some of these substances are more addictive than the drugs they are designed to mimic, as they bypass the normal pathways and blockers in the brain.

At the time of this book going to press in the UK, synthetic cannabinoids have been re-categorized as a Class B drug under the Misuse of Drugs Act. Mephedrone had previously been included in the same act as a Class B stimulant drug. These synthetic substances now have criminal controls applied to them. There are still other synthetic substances under the Psychoactive

Substances Act that are legal to possess and use but illegal to sell, import/ export. *Strange!*

Drug by Type

Some drugs are legal to use, both prescribed and OTC medicines. Others are not, such as statutory illegal/internet/black market prescription, etc. Arrest and conviction can lead to a variety of problems for the misuser/abuser. Many discussions have occurred with regard to the zero-tolerance approach to substances being found in a donor's sample as opposed to the issue of the donor being impaired by the use of substances or alcohol. To be clear, there are a variety of definitions of impairment; two in relation to substance misuse may be

1. **Impairment** is the state of being diminished, weakened or damaged, mentally or physically. It includes a detrimental impact on cognitive abilities.
2. **Cognitive** abilities are reduced or disturbed in relation to the mental processes of perception, memory, judgement and reasoning, as contrasted with emotional and volitional processes.

With regard to impairment and the judgement of how someone appears to be impaired, I have already recommended that for workplace situations avoid the term impairment and refer to a visible impairment or question the individual's cognitive abilities to reflect a particular incident, etc. Proving the existence of impairment issues where none are visible is, as mentioned earlier, an area fraught with a great many issues.

It is sufficient to say in your policy that at the time a request for a drug or alcohol test is made, the employee needs to be free from drugs (above the recognized country cut-off levels) or alcohol below an agreed cut-off. Your policy needs to reflect the wide- and narrow-window test mediums. See Chapters 2 and 3.

It can be and at times is argued that the use of illicit substances is a criminal offence and by the very nature of criminality requires a zero-tolerance approach under a variety of civil and criminal legislations. In the workplace it is the illegal use that is used to challenge the 'user's' subsequent integrity and the application of policy and T&Cs of employment. The police in society have the power, rightly or wrongly, to caution those who possess small amounts of illegal drugs, regardless of Class A, B or C. Over the years the amount and range of drugs the police can caution for seems to have increased. The punitive reactions from within the Criminal Justice System

(CJS) cannot be replicated by the employer, who will undoubtedly fall foul of those same laws as well as others, to say nothing of the threat of the removal of their insurance cover/claim, so critical to business operations.

What about the misuse or the side effects of legally provided substances, either prescribed or OTC and subsequently used to self-medicate for a different ailment from the one for which it was originally intended? Is a zero-tolerance approach appropriate when dealing with legally obtained prescribed medications or substances? The answer is no; it does require a different approach. Since the UK drug driving laws were introduced in March 2015, to date, arrests and convictions for being unfit to drive due to the misuse of illegal substances have risen alarmingly, more than 800%. In the UK workplace there is an increasing and alarming use of black-market prescription medications, as alluded to earlier.

Example

An employee, whose role is to drive a large heavy goods vehicle fails a Point of Care (POC) drug test and a subsequent BTL drug test is sent for analysis. He failed the POC test and tested positive for opiates; the subsequent laboratory analysis also was positive for tramadol and cocaine above the legal cut-off. The cocaine had been bought in the pub. The tramadol had been legally prescribed some months earlier for a back injury, not used, but subsequently the individual self-medicated from the stockpile of tramadol for an ear infection.

Many UK households contain a range of unused, stockpiled prescribed medications in a cupboard somewhere, especially in the homes of elderly persons who have experienced a range of ailments and accumulated unused repeat medications over the years.

It is imperative that employees keep their prescription, part B, for presentation at the time a drug test is requested in the workplace or as soon as practicable thereafter. It is imperative that the employer has visibility of any part B of a job applicant's relevant medication or an employee's relevant medication that may produce a positive reading above the cut-off level on a range of specific test substances, usually provided by a toxicology/analytical facility.

Considerations

1. What stance should the employer take with regard to legal and illegal substance misuse/abuse?

2. What are the responsibilities of the user of legal substances in relation to impairment of cognitive abilities as an employee?
3. What are the culpabilities or responsibilities of the employer or manager?
4. What is the difference between culpability and responsibility, and to whom should it be applied once the difference is identified?
5. How should these subjects be incorporated into a company SAMP, POT, EAP or T&Cs of employment?
6. What are the dangers/impact areas of workplace substance and alcohol misuse?

The dangers of substance misuse (Drug by Type) may also depend on

- The more drug that is ingested into the human body the greater the danger.
- Taking too much of a depressant drug can lead to a fatal overdose.
- Taking a large dose of a stimulant drug can lead to panic attacks, or even in extreme cases, psychotic behaviour (where all sense of reality is lost).
- Taking a large dose of a hallucinogenic drug may lead to disturbing experiences.
- Taking a high dose or a cocktail of drugs can lead to a lack of co-ordination and increase the likelihood of an overdose which can be fatal.
- Taking too much codeine will lead to a codeine tolerance where people will crave more because they are getting less and less conversion of the morphine from what they take. This is also true of many analgesic drugs that are opiate based.

Other dangers:

How often the drug is taken. The more often a drug is taken, the greater the risks to health, particularly if the user's body hasn't had time to recover or the tolerance has taken the risk of organ failure to a dangerous/imminent level. The concern here is taking so much drug over a period of time that the body builds a tolerance to a substance from which it is very difficult to recover. The body's tolerance to a drug usually develops when the user(s) is not converting as much of the drug to achieve a high, or in the case of an opiate the treatment of pain relief has fallen significantly below the need to take the drug in the first place. Taking the same amount of drug needed with high tolerance levels can cause an overdose, especially with drugs like heroin.

Other things in drugs (adulterants). Many illegal drugs, especially in powder or pill form, have other drugs, substances or bulking agents mixed with them. These can change the effect of the drugs and contribute to the dangers. Some cutting agents are actually passed off as the drug they are purporting to be. A person may not always necessarily be taking a drug at all; there is no quality control or honesty in crime and there are a great many counterfeit situations in the distribution of illegal and prescribed drugs.

Mixing drugs. Combining drugs can produce unpredictable and sometimes dangerous effects; mixtures of depressant drugs can be very dangerous. Many users have reported drug overdoses involving mixtures of alcohol and tranquillizers or opiates. Some users of stimulant drugs will take a depressant drug to counteract the stimulant effect, e.g., 'uppers' and 'downers'.

Drug dangers also vary with the method used to take them

Injection is a high-risk method because it is difficult to know how much is being taken. Injection also carries the risk of infection by a blood-borne virus (BBV) if any injecting equipment is shared or discarded. A high profile has been given to HIV, but there are also risks from hepatitis B and C, both of which are potentially very serious blood-borne diseases. There is some merit to the use or development of so-called shooting galleries to reduce the reuse or discarding of used/infected injecting paraphernalia; needle exchanges are also good countermeasures. I am not sure that the taxpayer is happy with the on-cost of a shooting gallery where free diamorphine is provided. There have been workplace situations in which a user has injected in a restroom and ruptured a vein. What countermeasures do you have in place for first aid, first responder or cleaning of a scene that may be infected with BBV issues?

Eating or drinking a drug can be risky if people take a large amount at one time, knowingly or otherwise. The effects tend to be slow in onset but once they occur it is too late to do anything about it. Examples are drinking too much alcohol in a short space of time or eating a lump of cannabis with a high THC content. In such cases people can suddenly feel very drunk or stoned and become extremely disorientated. Alcohol is a drug, a depressant, yet many use it to become happy and uninhibited or when they are already depressed. There is a need for further education and leadership training regarding the impact of substance and alcohol misuse in the workplace.

Snorting drugs like amphetamine or cocaine powder up the nose on a regular basis can lead to damage of the nasal membranes, although this risk may have been exaggerated on occasion. Snorting drugs can produce a more intense and rapid result from the drug being ingested, which in due course can significantly increase the rate of addiction and also the user's risk of overdose or of health issues related to misuse of or dependency on other substances.

Squirting and inhaling solvents such as glues, gases and aerosols are done using a number of dangerous methods. Squirting solvents into a large plastic bag and then placing the bag over the head has led to death by suffocation. Squirting aerosols or butane straight down the throat or into the nostrils has led to death through freezing of the airways. Regardless of the way in which solvents or noxious fumes are delivered into the body, all are still dangerous. It is worth noting that in the UK glues, gases and aerosols are now controlled under the Psychoactive Substances Act.

Smoking a drug is also a dangerous method of ingestion which may be more dependent on the type of drug being smoked and regularity of use. Regular smoking can damage the respiratory system, especially if the drug is smoked with tobacco, as is often the case with cannabis. The smoking of crack cocaine and chasing the dragon (smoking heroin) are more dangerous because of the type of drug and relevant purity.

The Individual Using

There are many reasons why people start using/misusing/abusing substances, whether illegal, legally prescribed or black market medicines, alcohol or psychoactive substances. Many people have never experienced a dependency of any sort. It can be very hard for these people to understand and grasp the reasons behind substance misuse and dependency, if they even identify their own dependency or tolerance to medications/substances.

With drug misuse/abuse becoming cheaper and more prevalent, it's now common for a variety of commentators to examine the topic in more depth and look for the reasons why people misuse/abuse drugs, substances and or alcohol. More legislation is introduced every year that impacts responsibility and culpability for an employer taking no action or taking the wrong action. For the employer who engages the correct countermeasures the problem is measurable and therefore manageable.

The paragraphs that follow are the internet commentary of a tragic situation in which a family member died of a drug overdose and are a powerful reminder of the circumstances that can occur from the misuse/abuse of substance(s). These nine situations highlight some of the issues as to why people may start to misuse/abuse substances and alcohol.

1. **People suffering from anxiety, bipolar disorder, depression or other mental health issues use drugs and alcohol to ease their suffering.**
   Mental illness and general wellbeing are such a burden for some people, who will try just about anything to relieve the anxiety or pain. Drugs or alcohol can temporarily make that person feel 'normal' again, just like they remember feeling in the past. Mental illness is frightening for the individual experiencing it, so they are afraid to go to a doctor, workmate, friend or family member for help and instead turn to drugs or alcohol to try and solve the problem on their own.

2. **People see family members, friends, role models or entertainers using drugs and rationalize that they can too.**
   It's very easy to think that drug and alcohol use can be handled and controlled, especially if they see others they know doing the same thing. It can become easy to rationalize, such as: 'My friend's been doing this for a couple years and he seems fine to me.' Entertainment and music are full of drug references and that can add to the rationalization that drug use is OK sometimes. Individuals with a family history of drug or alcohol abuse are far more likely to develop an addiction than an individual with no family background of addiction. The public is under a voracious attack from drinks manufacturers and advertising companies to enjoy their products. At what cost?

3. **People become bored and think drugs will help.**
   Boredom is a big factor in drug abuse, especially among teens and young adults. People in this age bracket generally don't have bills, jobs and all the stresses that go along with adulthood. So it's easier to become bored and want to try something new and exciting. Drug use is often thought of as a way to escape the mundane world and enter an altered reality.

4. **People think drugs will help relieve stress.**
   Our modern world is full of new strains and stresses that humans have never experienced in the past. Although many things in life are now easier than ever, the burdens are also very high. Simply having a family, maintaining a household and holding a job are huge stress factors.

Some drugs are viewed as a means of relaxation – a way to calm the storm in your mind. Although drugs can be very effective at doing that, there can be serious side effects.

5. **People think if a drug is prescribed by a doctor, it must be OK.**
It is easy for an individual to rationalize using a drug because it came from a doctor. The thinking goes like this: 'It was prescribed to someone I know for the same problem I am having, so it makes sense it should work for me too.' The dangerous part about this rationalization is that it can lead to mixing of drugs, overdose, unintended side effects and/or dependency.

6. **People get physically injured and unintentionally get hooked on prescribed drugs.**
The people at risk for this are physical labourers, the elderly, and anyone with pre-existing injuries. Some people are born with chronic pain due to a variety of disabilities and others sustain an injury at some time in their life. Doctors then prescribe drugs for the intended condition and a person can quickly build a dependency. Especially if that drug is making them feel better, they rationalize that it must be OK to keep taking it, which can result in dependency.

7. **People use drugs to cover painful memories in their past.**
Many people go through extremely traumatic events in their life, many times as children, and turn to drugs to cover the disturbing memories. Children are extremely susceptible to trauma, whether physical or emotional, and those feelings can haunt them into adulthood. These people could benefit from working with psychologists to help repair the damage to their mind. Drugs usually only intensify the issue.

8. **People think drugs will help them fit in.**
When hanging out with friends, it's easy for people to want to fit in and seem like one of the crew. If others are drinking or doing drugs, it's very likely for someone to fall into that trap. Peer pressure can be a tremendous force causing someone to try things they would normally not try on their own.

9. **People chase the high they once experienced.**
Ask anyone who has tried drugs and they will tell you that it is one of the best feelings of their life. The highs from drugs are so much more extreme than regular everyday joys because most drugs overload the pleasure sensors in a person's brain. Once a person feels this extreme pleasure, it's common for that person to become hooked on a drug

simply to chase the initial high they once felt. As we all know, this is a vicious cycle that is extremely difficult to break. The highs are equally as powerful as the lows felt when coming off of the drugs.

Everyone has a different defence mechanism or breaking point where they descend into an irrational response that may be out of character or their activity visibly changes their normal character.

Within the workplace there is a need to examine training methods for managers and awareness sessions so that employees can better identify and deal with a wide variety of substance and alcohol misuse situations. Workplace poster campaigns should not be ignored, as they form an important part of the Hall & Angus support mechanism to our clients and their workforce. The more educated people are about the problems and side effects, the better positioned they are to prevent the problem altogether.

The Location Used

The place where drugs are used and what people are doing at the time they are used can influence how dangerous they already are or may become. For example, some people take drugs in isolated or remote locations. The side effects or ramifications of accidents or overdose (OD) are much more likely to be compounded in remote locations, especially where response time is a critical factor for an emergency clinical intervention. This is especially true if the user is intoxicated or under the influence of substances and their visible and invisible judgement or compromised cognitive abilities prevent them from protecting themselves or others from harm or injury. If anything does go wrong, it is unlikely help will be readily at hand or that an ambulance/first responder could easily be called to quickly locate and manage an individual's problems.

Even if the location is not in itself inherently dangerous there may be other types of risks associated with the place of use, such as in flight, at sea, in mining, driving vehicles, using machinery or simply being a non-user who is in an environment where substance misuse and criminality surrounds them and is a disruptive element to their safety, e.g., the dangers of the impairment of their colleagues and so on.

Using or taking drugs into the workplace has led to the dismissal of a substantial number of employees, with drastic effects on their lives and families, as well as leading to their isolation within the community, and more.

The other issue is the circulation of these employees in the employment pool. If you do not have a substance misuse countermeasure in place you may be employing someone else's reject, and in the future your insurer will be looking more and more at this when claims are made. Workplace substance and alcohol misuse locations vary and are not restricted to:

- Toilets
- Smoking areas
- Car parks, in and outside of vehicles
- Immediately outside of the perimeter fence-line of the company
- Isolated areas
- Store cupboards
- In plain view and more

There are also issues with regard to concealment of substances and paraphernalia used to sell, administer or ingest the drugs while in the workplace. It is this area that will require a search and seizure policy within the SAMP and should include regular overt and covert searches of potential concealment/usage areas.

It is clear that driving a car, forklift, truck, bus, train or other ride on equipment or operating machinery while under the influence of illegal drugs or misuse of prescribed or OTC substances can greatly increase the risks of accidents in the workplace for the user and colleagues alike. Substance misuse can lower inhibitions, damage cognitive abilities, increase the likelihood of sexual encounters, etc. In society and the workplace safer sex, e.g., the conscious use of condoms/birth control, can be much more difficult if one or both parties concerned are under the influence of substances or alcohol. The risks of unwanted pregnancy or HIV and other sexually transmitted infections could increase if people have sex while under the influence of substances or alcohol.

Surveys have found that many people have had sexual encounters while under the influence of alcohol and or drugs. Work colleagues fare no better and such issues often lead to workplace intimidation, increased criminal activity, sexual and other harassment, crime, absenteeism, high staff turnaround, bullying, etc. All have an on-cost or a negative impact on the employer as well as the individual who becomes a victim.

Another danger is that of people overexerting themselves in or away from the workplace when using ecstasy, amphetamines and other stimulants, strong painkillers and even high-energy drinks. These substances give a temporary release of energy or pain relief and are often used in clubs while someone is dancing non-stop for long periods. In some situations people have danced for hours without a break in hot, crowded environments. They run the risk of becoming dehydrated and suffering heat exhaustion. In some cases this can be very dangerous and has led to a number of deaths. 'Chilling out', taking a break from dancing, cooling off and sipping or drinking water or fruit juice at regular intervals (not alcohol as it further dehydrates the user) reduces these risks. Also, be aware of the risk of overhydrating, which can also be fatal.

In the workplace stimulants are used to get people through a long day or when working in extreme conditions/pressures. High-energy caffeine drinks are not just misused in the workplace but also affect children who see adults using the drink and the rapacious advertising campaigns of manufacturers of the drinks. Caffeine is a regulated substance in Australia and some other countries, and it's time the UK took a stance on caffeine consumption, especially by children. The other issue is taking drugs such as painkillers to be fit for work. The relevant questions are the following:

- Are you actually fit for work? (Fiduciary Duty UK)
- Is it that you cannot afford to miss work, despite the injury/illness?

There are many possible risks and dangers involved when misusing/abusing drugs, especially when mixing them with alcohol or taking a cocktail drug approach to misuse/abuse. There are a great many issues for the user who may have an underlying health deficiency to consider, worse still if they do not know about *any* undiagnosed underlying health issue.

In addition, people may experience interpersonal problems with drug and alcohol misuse because of other individuals' perceptions and responses to them. Examples include conflict in family and other personal relationships, getting expelled from school/college or dismissed at work, acquiring a criminal record, getting into debt or criminality to pay for drugs, feeding a dependency of any kind or violence associated with drug abuse/dealing and much more. The increased and varied stresses on modern-day living are constantly changing.

Everything in modern life is about rapid development, rapid change, rapid wealth and mass media. Despite this accessibility to mass media there are still a great many people who are misinformed about the dangers of their actions with regard to substance and alcohol misuse or believe there are no consequences to their actions, as they will be looked after by a variety of emergency services or specialists. The fact is, without knowledge on the subject, how can you make a considered judgement about your own safety and the safety of those around you, especially with regard to substance and alcohol misuse?

To understand potential risks and dangers you will need to think about:

'The Drug by Type', 'the Individual Using' and 'the Location Used'.

Some reasons why people get involved with drugs

Accidental, Anxiety, Availability

Because it's daring, because it's fun, because peers are using, because they want to, because it's been said to be good, Bereavement, Blot-out problems, Bonding, Boredom, Born dependent, Brought up in drug culture, Buzz

Celebration, Cheap form of entertainment, Complements food, Conditioning, Confidence builder, Cultural standing, Cultural influence, Curiosity, Credibility

Depression, Desensitized to one – start on another, De-stressor, Don't know any better, Drown sorrows

Effect, Enhance performance-work-sport-sex-study, Escapism, Excitement, Experimentation

Family, Family history, Family environment factors, Forbidden fruit, Forced dependency, Freebies

Genetic vulnerability, Glamour, Grooming

Health, High self-esteem

Injury, Isolation

Juvenile outlook

Knowing other users, Known effects

Lack of knowledge or understanding of risks or dangers, Life circumstances/experiences, Low self-esteem

Maintaining standards, Marketing advertisements, Medicinal, Mistake

No willpower, No self-esteem

Obesity, Others use

Pain relief, Peer pressure, Pleasure

Quick fix to problems

Rebellion, Recreational, Risk taking

Shift work, Social reasons, Spiked drink or food, Stress

Thinking they won't become addicted, To get high–to get low, To help relax, To provoke alternative thinking, Trend – trendy

Unable to deal with problems

Vulnerability to drug use, Vulnerable in society

Wanting to be in control

X-Factor

Young and daring

Zero outlook, Zest for trying something different, Zig-Zagging across different drug groups

Some behavioural or emotional indicators of substance and alcohol misuse

Aggressive body language, Argumentative, Agitation, Anxiety

Babbling, Bullying and intimidating demeanour, Boisterous behaviour as an individual or in groups

Changes in friendship circles, Changes in hobbies or interest, Changes in sex drive, Constant chatter-talking rubbish

Disrupted eating patterns, Depression

Extreme Happiness

Fidgeting, Forgetfulness

Giggling, Gouching out

Hallucinations, Hyperactivity

Increase in confidence, Incoherent, Irrational behaviour

Juvenile behaviour, Judgemental

Knife carrying, Key changes in demeanour

Little/no appetite or munchies, Lack of concentration, Loss of spark

Mood swings, Money problems

Neglect of dependents including pets, New peer group

Out of character behaviour

41

Poor co-ordination, Paranoia

Quality of life or lack thereof

Rebellion, Rude

Secretive-furtive behaviour, Slurred speech, Spaced out/unaware, Staying in bed, Stealing, Suicidal thoughts

Theft, Thoughtlessness

Unexplained absences

Verbal diarrhoea

Withdrawal from usual social setting

Yawning

Zombie effect, Zonked out

There are many more behavioural or emotional indicators, which will become evident in different ways depending on the circumstances that have been highlighted or the user's situation socially or in the workplace. In the workplace managing an intervention and providing the appropriate support package is critical to treating the individual with dignity while protecting the company and the individual's colleagues from unnecessary harm or humiliation.

It is usually difficult to tell if people are misusing drugs, whether for the first time or occasionally. Many of the 'signs' and 'symptoms' are just like the everyday signs of a variety of issues. Regular and chaotic drug abusers are usually more easily visible and require a serious level of protracted intervention and treatment.

In some instances of substance misuse/abuse, there may be no visible signs and symptoms. It is important to remember that trying to spot signs and symptoms of substance and alcohol misuse is no substitute for good communication, training and self-referral mechanisms.

Example

Dilated pupil/Pin point pupil
There may be a range of issues that cause these two often used indicators of substance or alcohol misuse. As with any indicator there is a need to examine the specific circumstances in which the individual is being assessed. Considering an accumulation of issues or circumstances that are being investigated is the best way forward.

Chapter summary

This chapter has outlined some of the basic considerations, situations and legislations that the employer and the management team need to balance against substance and alcohol misuse/abuse and its correlation to criminality. It presents a general picture; when managing workplace situations and individuals, each situation will also have its own peculiarities. While on the face of it a zero-tolerance approach to the criminality of substance misuse/abuse appears to be a straightforward dismissal, I hope this chapter will cause pause for thought. The actions taken against an employee who deals or traffics drugs in the workplace are straightforward. The person who is a victim, reluctant user, self-inflicted or otherwise, in many cases deserves a second chance and at the very least the consideration of support from the employer.

An employer invests much time and energy in the development of the leadership team and the employees within the business. To throw it all away on the basis of a person's misuse (not abuse) of substances and alcohol may be a false economy. The cost of new recruitment, training, management and upskilling will likely be higher than the rehabilitation or limited but managed intervention of a full-time/long-term employee. The management of human assets needs to be conducted with dignity, not with humiliation.

Do

1. Think about your company's operations and country-specific legislative obligations.
2. Think about your risk exposure by not having a substance and alcohol misuse referral/management capability.
3. Think about your employees, who have their own pressures to get by in life. What can you do to help?
4. Think about who in your management team has culpability regarding managing substance and alcohol misuse/abuse issues and the ramifications to the company and the individual of failing in that culpability.
5. Think about who has responsibility and the training required to understand and deliver that responsibility.
6. Think about the range of drugs now available in society and close to your own regional or country demographics.
7. Think about the big picture of substance and alcohol misuse: there is more to consider than you may think.

8. Think about the current state of society. Can your actions in the work-place help change the negatives and enhance the positives while also having a positive impact in the local community?
9. Think about your insurance responsibilities. The insurance companies are certainly thinking about their exposure.
10. Do challenge your insurance premiums where you have installed a range of documented countermeasures.

Do not

1. Ignore your culpability or the hidden threat of substance and alcohol misuse that is waiting to catch you out, within a range of criminal and civil legislations.
2. Ignore your responsibility to train your managers and employees. They will help you protect your business and make it more efficient and profitable.
3. Ignore the need to communicate substance and alcohol misuse govern-ance across your whole business. Failure to communicate will lead to a great many other failings.
4. Believe the problem does not exist in your company.
5. Believe you will lose too many staff by introducing a Programme of Testing.

'Ignore the threat and consequences of doing nothing and not being prepared for everything'

– Trevor Hall

2 | Drug testing in the workplace
How does it work?

Introduction

No matter where you are in the world, no matter who your provider is, no matter which equipment you select to use for workplace substance and alcohol testing, all will need the consideration of this chapter to build a robust and effective Programme Of Testing (POT).

In this book you will keep seeing references to the Substance and Alcohol Misuse Policy (SAMP), POT and Employee Assistance Programme (EAP); these three areas are the main elements within the construction of your workplace Substance and Alcohol Misuse Management Programme (SMMP) and the company's governance of it. They will all need to be embedded into T&Cs of employment and other areas of business management.

Spend some time on the following:

- Consider what you want to achieve from workplace test mediums and question which are most appropriate.
- Consider which are the best test mediums for your company's operations with the least disruption and with the best protection for your business and the protection of your employees.
- Understand what test mediums can and cannot do; be sure your analytical laboratory is accredited around those test mediums.
- Understand how your chosen provider(s) will support you within your robust and legally defensible SAMP, POT and EAP.
- Work with your analytical provider or a specialist provider to ensure your staff members are trained in an awareness of substance misuse and the

nature of your chosen test mediums, especially how they will be applied in the workplace pre- and post-employment.

- Set your supply chain Service Level Agreement (SLA) and Key Performance Indicators (KPIs) from within this and other chapters.
- The SLA and KPIs with regard to your supplier should identify penalties incurred when the supplier fails to meet your or their own standards.
- Your chosen analytical provider, which may also be your main supplier, should have clear SLA and KPIs for sample turnaround times; anything more than 48 hours from receipt at the laboratory is just not good enough for workplace situations. Less than 48 hours is even better. The standard met by the Hall & Angus sister company, TOX247 Ltd in the UK, is a maximum of 48 hours turnaround, with 82% of all samples being turned around in 24 hours.

You will have your own reasons for testing in the workplace; the foregoing are just some operational considerations. Be sure you are embarking on the journey of workplace substance and alcohol misuse testing from an exacting research basis. Hopefully this chapter and book will help in that process.

> *'Do not believe that you have a strong deterrent because you employ a weak Point of Care drug test on a random basis in your workplace. You will have a stronger deterrent if you have a robust policy and T&Cs of employment which reflect a robust Programme of Testing applied to the right circumstances.'*
>
> – Trevor Hall

Drug testing in society is very much restricted to certain situations: drug driving legislations, paternity testing, legal cases, healthcare, criminal justice system, sport and so on. Society relies on legislations and those who enforce them to manage illegal and legal substance misuse with an ever-decreasing menu of resources that are very often overstretched but with dedicated people left to manage such issues successfully in today's times. Government strategies seem to be disjointed and send mixed messages from a range of departments and regulatory bodies or lobbying organizations, police commissioners and chief constables, etc. *What are the relevant agencies in your country and what is their approach on such matters?*

Debates continue around the legalization of certain illegal drugs, especially cannabis. There are some benefits to be derived from refined cannabinoids that have clinical applications. The same is true, however, of other substances such as opium, cocaine and amphetamine, to name just a few. As there is no outcry to legalize these drugs, why would we therefore make the argument to legalize high-strength unrefined cannabis?

Throughout this and other chapters, there are pictures of common UK drugs, paraphernalia, test equipment and other informative subjects. People are proactive in what they want to achieve or avoid within or outside of a range of legislations, policies and guidelines, including the misuse of substances and alcohol. Legislations, policies and guidelines therefore have to be reactive but with the vision to manage just about any situation that will stress-test its ability to provide formal judgement and management, with a consistent response to proportionate and appropriate consequences.

In the case of substance misuse, the situation is always fluid around new drugs, whether legal, designer or otherwise illegal. It is all compounded by the proactivity of non-conforming people who remain a hidden threat within the workplace as well as society. Employers are better positioned to manage that hidden threat than most countermeasures applied across society. In addition, if the governments of the day desire a UK culture change then that can be achieved quite easily by helping employers, who across the public and private sectors are able to influence the attitudes/culture of more than 35 million UK employees. There are other areas that can be applied to assist governments, e.g. insurance companies, regulatory bodies, education establishments and so on, all need to work together. *What is the working population in your country that can be influenced to help promote changes in society or to change a negative culture?*

So, how do we define what is substance misuse and why does it have to be managed in the workplace in a manner that is different from that in society? If the first chapter has convinced you of the need to manage people and circumstances, this chapter is a part of how that can be achieved.

Common test mediums

Drugs are stored in and expelled from the human body in different ways and through different organs; the route that will be examined and analysed depends on which test medium you choose. The more common test mediums are the following, in our order of priority.

Cut head and body hair/fingernail clipping analysis (wide-window testing)

Drug metabolites and cross-reactivity compounds are deposited through the bloodstream into the hair and fingernails of those who misuse substances and alcohol. Hair is a wide-window (90 days to 6 months or more) detection method and can be used in multiple situations, the most obvious being in pre-employment, where the problem can be stopped by not allowing entry in the workplace to begin with.

Saliva analysis (narrow-window testing)

With saliva, substances are recovered from the glands in the mouth and throat that have also been deposited via the bloodstream. Saliva is a narrow-window (0–36 hours) test medium and as such is a closer test to blood than other test mediums and is best suited for the invisible impairment argument.

Breath screening (recent use of alcohol)

With breath, we examine a deep lung sample, again via the blood circulating in the respiratory system. There are a wide variety of cut-offs for drink driving across a wide variety of sector and legislation-specific enforcements. *What are they in your country?*

Urine analysis (narrow-window testing, except for cannabis in certain circumstances)

With urine, drugs are ingested and expelled from the body through various organs, such as the bladder, liver and kidneys. Some drugs, however, are also stored in fatty tissues for longer periods than others; this is true of cannabis, which in itself is a sticky metabolite.

Hair and fingernail clippings provide a wide-window historical examination of a person's use of substances; the other mediums show more recent use. More importantly, hair and fingernail clippings also provide proof that substances have *not been used* for a protracted period of time. This situation is very important to those risk positions and pre-employment protocols of employees where the risk element is investigated with regard to non-use as opposed to recent or regular misuse.

At Hall & Angus we have very definite ideas around proactive and reactive substance and alcohol misuse testing. We have very grave concerns about the use of Point Of Care (POC) instant testing to prevent people from working, to ban contractors from certain companies/contracts for life, or being used to dismiss people from employment based on results of what is a **non-evidential screening device**, which includes breath alcohol screening devices which are also, in the UK, **non-evidential screening devices.**

A Point Of Care device is a fixed panel device of limited testing capability that is non-evidential. The only affirmative action that can be taken is to suspend an employee on full pay or take the wrong action for all the wrong reasons. It is another on-cost and another step in the process that very often can be eliminated. When conducting random testing use a rapid turnaround back to laboratory saliva test. That way you have evidential value on the result and until you get the result you do not have to suspend employees from a random testing programme.

We have further concerns that the current recognized workplace instant and laboratory metabolite cut-offs are not fit for UK purposes when applied to current levels of prescription medications used by employees under the guidance of their GP. This is especially true with regard to opiates and other strong painkillers such as tramadol, codeine, gabapentin, pregabalin and so on. Many drugs used beyond the manufacturer's recommendations will on accumulation provide positive test results. This situation requires closer examination and a serious review of not just cut-offs, but also of whether or not there is a ready need to examine a prescribed medication dosage against an individual. The body's metabolization of certain compounds will be clouded once the donor has developed a dependency, e.g. in opiate misuse, where the user is continuously prescribed a medication which is designed for short-term use.

There are many occasions in which potential employees/contractors attend the workplace for induction or even pre-employment testing and are subsequently prohibited from work because an instant test device showed a presumptive positive for opiates, despite the production of a relevant prescription. The opiate panel is the gatekeeper to identifying heroin users. At this stage heroin can be identified only when a sample is sent for analysis to an accredited laboratory. Employers are reluctant to use a Back To Laboratory (BTL) confirmation test on a potential employee, due mainly to cost, but also the fact they can reject the application or induction candidate as a non-employee. Alternatively, potential employees might present a prescription for high doses of prescribed medications that are not the subject of the test. There are two issues here with regard to prescription medications in the workplace:

1. Does the employee or potential employee have a current prescription in their name for an opiate-based/other medication that may have debilitating side effects? If that is the case, the issue is: when or even if they submit a BTL sample, currently it may still test positive above a very low cut-off, not relevant to their prescription. *Problem!*
2. If the employee or potential employee cannot produce a prescription in their name but has used black market opiates or another's prescription drug or it is decided they have used a Class A, B or C prescribed drug as identified in the Misuse of Drugs Act (Compounds List), then any of these situations in the workplace is a ZERO tolerance situation around criminality. *No Problem!*

There is, however, another issue often discovered and that revolves around self-medication by a person who has medications that were legally prescribed for a previous injury/symptom and then subsequently misuses from old stockpiled medications.

Example

A person was injured sometime in the past and was prescribed tramadol in a large dose. That injury/symptom has since passed but the person continues at some later date to fall back onto their stockpile of strong painkillers for a self-diagnosed, self-medicated and unrelated injury/symptom. They subsequently mix this medication with alcohol to achieve a high, and the original prescription as reference material to the legal prescribing/use of the drug has long since been thrown away.

Over-the-counter medications

There are also over-the-counter (OTC) medications that are below prescribing levels, but when deliberately mixed with alcohol they become an impairment/dependency situation. All situations need to be managed in the workplace and advised to the individual who has fallen foul of misuse/

dependency issues. Some users will trawl multiple pharmacies to achieve a target on stockpiling lower strength drugs, usually painkillers.

Additional considerations

We already know that some GPs breach manufacturers' guidelines for the duration an individual should be prescribed certain strong painkillers and other drugs such as Benzodiazepines. What we do not know is how prolific this problem is. We are not certain of the insurance implications between GP and manufacturer if this is challenged in a workplace dismissal/injury-related incident or even a civil claim. This situation has led to the need to conduct a controlled study of:

1. The impact of prescribed medications in the workplace.
2. The correlation to analytical cut-offs for legally prescribed medication in the UK.
3. The associated prescribing regimes from GPs as opposed to the guidelines from drug manufacturers.

The study considerations

There is a need for the study to examine and report on:

1. How many employees come to work despite the need to take debilitating medications?
2. How many employees continue to come to work because they cannot afford to be away from work despite the need to take debilitating medications?
3. How many are actually prevented from working because of their prescribed medications?
4. What is the size and impact of the UK black market sale of prescribed medications outside of GP or prescription control? *What is the nature of this problem in your country?*
5. How many people are self-medicating prescribed/controlled drugs from old prescriptions?
6. What are the experiences of employees prescribed large doses of debilitating medications immediately as opposed to gradually?

7. What are the UK implications under the various legislations that included the Health Safety at Work Acts and Regulations and the new Insurance Act invoked on employers in 2016? *How does this apply in your country?*

8. How should the workplace manage an employee in the following situations:
   - What is the impact to the employer and the employee in the process of increasing dosages of debilitating medications in the early stages of prescribing, or when the body's ingestion is still being measured for reaction/side effects? Is the employee fit for work or not?
   - Once the maximum dosage is prescribed, what is the impact on the individual's subsequent or continued employability in their existing role, or a reasonable adjustment, if one is available?

9. There is also a need for a debate with specialist physicians who deal with the management of prescribed medication (especially pain relief) dependency and the manufacturer's approach to guidance regarding the drugs they deliver into the general market.

Until this Hall & Angus study is complete and comprehensively reported on, the workplace approach to managing illegal substances, managing illegal use of legal substances and managing prescription medications needs to be consistent, considered and appropriate, as outlined in this book.

Methodology

There should be a controlled approach to a workplace testing programme that sets standards concerning:

1. The protection of the donor's dignity and legal rights.
2. The elimination of humiliating full-pay suspension or being prevented from a work opportunity where no evidence of substance misuse exists, especially with regard to the use of non-evidential test devices.
3. A considered and consistent approach to managing
   - Illegal substances
   - Properly prescribed medications
   - Illegal use of legally prescribed/black market medications.
4. An examination and delivery of due diligence and risk management imposed on the employer and subsequently on the employee/contractor.

5. The protection of principal contractors targeted to manage substance and alcohol misuse issues under a variety of contracted circumstances.

6. The protection of subcontractors and their employees who are subject to principal contractor guidelines.

7. The setting of standards that are consistent, robust, fair, achievable and can be the minimum standard applied for the protection of all concerned.

8. A controlled management of alcohol testing in the workplace where the use of what is a legal substance is measured against a person's ability to drive a vehicle under the Road Traffic Act, which cannot be applied in the workplace. There needs to be more consideration as to how limits for alcohol misuse are set in the workplace. There is also a need to closely examine the application of any disciplinary process around alcohol.

In certain contract/tendering/compliance requirements the current number of drug groups identified in analytical services is too limited, and there is a need for these to be expanded, especially to cover drugs now identified in the drug driving regulations. Healthcare POC devices should not be used for workplace situations because of the limited panel of drugs and the different cut-offs for healthcare medications when compared against workplace cut-offs. The workplace POC device needs to include synthetic cannabinoids and benzodiazepines that are now part of the Misuse of Drugs Act and UK drug driving regulations, respectively. Under either legislation why would you test for tetrahydrocannabinol and not test for synthetic cannabinoids or benzodiazepines which have more debilitating side effects than low-volume usage of prescribed medications?

Suggested UK workplace panel for POC devices

The first suggestion is that the following panel of drugs be the minimum adopted for UK workplace pre-/post-employment POC devices:

1. Tetrahydrocannabinol (THC, cannabis)
2. Cocaine
3. Amphetamines
4. Methamphetamine (includes Ecstasy)
5. Benzodiazepines
6. Methadone
7. K2 (synthetic cannabinoids)

8. Ketamine
9. Opiates
10. Buprenorphine

Phencyclidine (PCP, 'angel dust') is most commonly used in the USA and is rarely found outside of the USA.

Other drug panels of 12 and 16 drug groups are available, and their use would be a company decision based on what the company is looking for, either full-time or occasionally throughout the year, or where there is a change in regional drug demographics or local intelligence is being applied.

In the UK, UKAS accredited analytical laboratories can expand the chosen drug panel on request when a sample is sent for BTL analysis. Alternatively, there are individual urine cassettes that can expand a limited saliva or urine panel to include additional substances such as:

1. Tramadol
2. Mephedrone
3. Pregabalin
4. Gabapentin
5. Many more depending on your provider

Testing should then be implemented in a flexible and considered approach with due deference to the specific incident/contract or need to test. The process should be incremental and in three stages.

1. **Preliminary or due diligence test (instant or BTL narrow-window testing)**
   Preliminary testing should not be the final stage of an employee testing package. The consideration here is that instant test devices are used to apply a modicum of due diligence. Preliminary testing is a methodology for:
   • Companies that test potential employees at short notice for short-term/temporary positions.
   • Principal contractors who are outsourcing specific short-term jobs/contract requirements to a specialist subcontractor.
   • POC testing of employees who are in or have completed company-sponsored rehabilitation programmes.
   Preliminary testing is an early-stage testing methodology that may require a lower-cost approach to testing, especially regarding volume and speed

of employment, usually testing on POC devices (instant testing). However, this does not mean that a BTL saliva/urine, narrow-window test should not be ruled out where advance pre-employment planning is a capability within any structured recruitment package.

2. **Standard test (BTL only, narrow or wide-window testing)**
Standard testing is not an area where instant test result devices are used. The standard test will always be a situation where only BTL analysis is applied, whichever test medium is used, wide or narrow-window. The standard test, like the preliminary test, can be upgraded depending on the role or position specific to an enhanced test. Standard testing should be used in the following circumstances:
- Testing staff who are being transitioned from a temporary contract to a full- time contract and where their previous test was provided on an instant preliminary test device.
- Using a BTL test medium as part of a structured *pre-employment* process in the following situations:
  (a) An enhanced company induction protocol requiring the signing of a variety of T&C documents in the process.
  (b) Where a job offer has been made and is subject to the candidate passing a substance misuse test or is part of a combined medical and substance misuse test.
- In random testing programmes, where a BTL application removes the need to suspend an employee on full pay.
- In for-cause testing where evidence is being sought as part of the for-cause investigation.

Standard testing is currently conducted where trackside rail-workers and other positions within transport routinely qualify to work in risk professions.

3. **Enhanced test (wide-window testing only)**
Enhanced testing raises the bar to the maximum level of testing, usually the examination via a wide-window test medium that shows the donor has *not used drugs for a protracted period of time* and is therefore less likely to become an occasional or regular substance misuser. The enhanced programme is also used to detect those who would be missed by a narrow-window/recent use test medium.

Many companies use hair analysis where they themselves provide a service delivery which is risk assessed as high or the company wants to have an enhanced reputation. Individual risk positions are mitigated by an annual test that proves *long-term abstinence from substance misuse*. A programme that also introduces a BTL narrow-window test for a random analysis programme eliminates the need for full-pay suspension from work. This is a two-fold benefit to companies:

1. It renders the Programme of Testing as more robust, and allied to a robust policy it represents a true deterrent in the workplace. Alternatively, a weak non-evidential POC device is looking for a needle in a haystack with a limited panel of drugs and the only outcome is a BTL test and the suspension of a staff member on full pay.
2. BTL testing is evidential and when used in a random programme it is more cost effective by eliminating the unnecessary full-pay suspension of employees.

Note: Any drug testing conducted in the workplace starts as a due diligence scenario, by the employer who wants to avoid the quantifiable on-cost of employing a substance misuser.

Note: The critical areas of standard and enhanced BTL testing are the rapid result turnaround of samples to within 24–48 hours of receipt at the laboratory. Make sure your provider has the correct SLA and can achieve a rapid sample turnaround time.

Explanation of instant, narrow and wide-window testing

1. Instant test results are provided on POC saliva, urine or alcohol breath test screening devices. They measure the recent use of some substances from hours to a few days, but do not provide evidence for use in tribunal or other litigation scenarios. This situation is non-evidential in every workplace scenario and indicates the need to start another process.
2. Narrow-window BTL testing includes the aforementioned time frame but the samples are sent to an analytical laboratory for the delivery of confirmation/negative evidence that can be produced in any disciplinary,

tribunal or other litigation. This where all workplace post-employment testing programmes should begin, eliminating the inappropriate stage 1.

3. Wide-window testing is BTL only and provides:
   - A historical examination of a person's substance misuse, whether casual, regular or chaotic use, and by what drug metabolite or cross-reactivity compound being searched for.
   - A historical examination of a person abstaining from substance misuse and therefore more likely not to misuse substances within their chosen lifestyle.
   - Wide-window test mediums include:
     1. Head hair cut as close to the scalp as possible, every centimetre thereafter providing an approximately 30-day window of detection/ abstinence.
     2. Cut body hair, which provides an approximately 3- to 9-month window of detection/abstinence, depending on the type of hair.
     3. Fingernail clippings, which produce an approximately 6-month window of detection/abstinence.
     4. Cut head hair can also be segmented to examine a person's integrity concerning their substance/alcohol misuse or claims of spiked drinks and other investigative situations.

As stated throughout this book, we identify with a 'prescription positive' scenario; as long as the donor has a prescription then there is little that can be done other than to monitor the employee's risk position in the workplace, monitor the employee's fitness around visible impairment due to the side effects of the drug prescribed, and guidance from the GP/drug manufacturer when there is a gradual increase in dosage dependent on the employee's reaction to a specific drug prescribed/prescribing regime, etc. Much more needs to be done to convince me that prescribed medication toxicology reporting is fit for purpose in the UK and elsewhere.

Where misuse of prescription drugs is identified, there is a need to manage the donor via the EAP, the GP and the toxicology laboratory. Employers and managers of workplace substance misuse issues need to take some time to consider the following:

- **Prescribed medication, off prescription, black market, etc.** The socio-economic impact of this problem has not been properly investigated and measured as a negative to society and ultimately the workplace. We are constantly reviewing this situation on behalf of our client base. The on-sale of repeat prescription drugs no longer used but infrequently reviewed by physicians has created a massive black market culture outside of GP and legislative control. Punitive actions are taken to stamp out this situation, which can cost lives and severely impact the positive life experiences of users and lead to a massive unchallenged on-cost to taxpayers, and to protect individuals in a great many other situations that require legislations, policies and guidelines. Situations such as road safety, safeguarding of children and so on can all be impacted by black market substance misuse. Painkillers and opiates are the main targets of this issue but there are other dependencies developing around the introduction of many new drugs. Remember, the possession and sale of legal substances normally controlled under a prescribing system can and do lead to the possession and/or trafficking of Class A, B or C drugs when the control of the prescription is bypassed. In the workplace this is a zero-tolerance scenario that can lead to dismissal or the denial of a position within the company at a pre-employment testing situation.

Discussion

As with the misuse of on-prescription medications there is a growing trend of black market use that has an impact on the workplace, companies are now having to manage this situation under a range of country-specific civil and criminal legislations. There is a need to also consider growing insurance countermeasures and the increasing trend to not pay out on insurance claims where substance misuse is considered a contributory factor to a claim. Insurers are constantly reviewing reasons to not pay claims or to reduce the risk of a claim in the first place, and workplace drug testing has a very large part to play in both situations. The use of prescribed medications off prescription is a growing problem for employers in many countries. An employer's actions in this area can have a very beneficial spin-off in the awareness of local or wider substance misuse and cultural change/management. What is the current position with regard to this subject in your company/country? What awareness training do you conduct? What are the black market drug use demographics in your local area/country?

- **Misuse of illegal drugs** as outlined in a variety of legislations is the easiest to manage in the workplace. For black market prescription drugs and the illegality around them, an employer has the easiest of solutions, 'A Zero Tolerance'. As an experienced international corporate and commercial investigator I have had to deal with a great many other negative issues regarding the misuse/possession/trafficking/organized crime infiltration of legal and illegal substances into the workplace. Once again, however, the employer can fall foul of a wide range of criminal and civil legislations by not dealing with the issues in the management and running of their business and the protection of those who work within it. Once again, the employer also has a significant part to play in the changing of local employment pool cultures and national culture change by overtly eliminating the use and misuse of substances in the workplace: *what a great SROI (Social Return On Investment)*. Current governments globally should take notice of what can be achieved on their behalf by employers and the support packages that can be mitigated within the workplace, with many incentives yet to be identified and discussed.

Discussion

Organized and opportunist crime infiltration into the workplace often revolves around illegal substance misuse/distribution, its exchange for stolen or diverted finished product, raw materials, illegal substances infiltrating the distribution network, blackmail, intimidation and so on. These issues apply mostly to global operations, but each country and local environment will have its own organized and opportunist criminal element operating in and around the workplace. What workplace countermeasures does your company have in place to identify and manage these situations within your country's law?

- **Designer drugs/new psychoactive substances (NPS)** that have few, if any, medicinal uses are a worry. In the UK they have been regulated under the Psychoactive Substances Act. *What is the situation in your country?* There appears to be little legal control being applied, with many NPS still easily available, openly sold and used, not just in society but also within the custodial penal system and the workplace. Once again, cost and commitment are essential issues to properly removing these negatives in society. The workplace, however, has a mandatory requirement in all of these substance misuse situations to take action of some sort immediately after they come to notice. Zero tolerance in the workplace is a must; anything less will negatively impact the workplace and the 35 million-plus UK people who work within it.

Discussion

The production of synthetic substances is designed to mimic the effects of illegal substances. There is some evidence that synthetic substances are more addictive than the drugs they are designed to mimic, reportedly in the way they bypass natural blockers in the brain. The internet, media and other commentators have many harrowing stories of those who fallen foul of the NPS epidemic. Where employees render themselves unfit for work through self-inflicted actions, what does your company do to cover these substances in a workplace substance misuse policy for those NPS drugs, some of which are legal to possess and use in the UK? What is the situation in your country?

- **Medicinal substances that are used for the wrong reasons** to facilitate the high of an illegal/legal substance or the commission of a crime. Gamma-hydroxybutyric acid (GHB), Rohypnol (roofies) and opiates have been used for all the wrong reasons and certainly not for what they were designed for – nitrous oxide (laughing gas) taken in tandem with alcohol and so on. For years medicinal preparations of drugs have been misused by those who have the knowledge of what the drug can do. Many unrefined street drugs contain the relevant metabolites to refine a drug for use in medications below a set of medicinal cut-offs, opium for morphine and other opioid pain killers, etc. Cocaine has uses in medications, as do amphetamines, ketamine, alkylnitrites and so on. These and many more have legal uses that when refined and delivered in measured doses can benefit the end user. It's the measured dose and the refinement that are the control, especially when used in medical procedures or prescription scenarios that are allegedly monitored and controlled. The debate around this topic is too large to be covered within this book, and will require the active contribution of a range of specialist experts. The application to workplace situations is, however, a consideration throughout all the chapters in this book.

Discussion

There is a need in the workplace to have a methodology to manage all of the aforementioned situations.

'The employer has a duty to manage situations that go unchallenged or are mismanaged in society. The employer's failure to do so can lead to prosecution under a range of criminal and civil legislations/

statutory requirements and the removal of critical insurance cover in certain situations.'

– Trevor Hall

What has your company done to mitigate these issues by policy, best practice and within criminal and civil legislations? What have you asked of your provider? Are they best qualified to support you? Are you properly trained and qualified to manage the company programme?

There are a great many other situations that can be applied to the misuse of a range of substances. Alcohol and its misuse in the workplace is covered in Chapter 5. Some alcohol misuse is covered in this chapter to indicate the way it can be detected and managed in the employer's strategy of dealing with alcohol misuse of varying degrees, especially in the manner they implement and use *test mediums*.

Test mediums: what they can and cannot do

A test medium is the particular device used to detect the drug metabolite or cross-reactivity compound. The test collection device is how and what is used to collect a controlled sample from a consenting donor applied under a set of T&Cs of employment and in line with the company's policy. The term test medium can be applied to hair, fingernail clippings, saliva, urine and deep lung breath. There are others but we would recommend the aforementioned test mediums in consideration of this book.

A POT is applied within the confines of a legally defensible policy. At the end of this chapter, there are two documents from the debate between POC testing (non-evidential instant test result) and BTL analysis (evidential confirmatory result). It's around this debate that you need to take serious consideration as to how your POT will be built/managed within your policy/recruitment protocols and what priority each takes in your chosen use. The other debate is about workplace substance misuse testing: compulsory versus voluntary. You may begin to see that substance and alcohol misuse testing is more compulsory than you think.

You will also need to consider the application of wide- and narrow-window test mediums in your SAMP, POT and EAP. You may also have sector-specific requirements to comply with.

What does hair analysis bring to the table?

(Time to collect, including Chain Of Custody (ChOC) 7–10 minutes per donor)

- Head hair, cut as close to the scalp as possible, provides an historical pattern of substance misuse as well as an historical pattern of non-use.
- Each half inch/centimetre of hair produces an approximately 30-day window of drug detection/history, whether proving positive or negative. A negative result on wide-window test mediums, as stated earlier, is equally as valuable as detecting a positive result, depending on what the client is looking to achieve.
- The maximum length cut in the workplace should be restricted to 1.5 inches/3 centimetres, which allows for equality between male and female hair length.
- Depending on the length, head hair can be segmented to examine each 30-day segment individually. This is often done when investigating spiked drink claims or to challenge the integrity of users who claim to be occasional as opposed to regular users, evidenced by individual segment analysis and concentration of drug metabolite recovered.
- Drugs stay in hair proportionate to use and the measure is therefore quantitative, especially when used in EAPs or examining the potential conversion of drug metabolites balanced against quantity used.
- Drugs stay in hair for as long as it takes for the hair to grow out post-cessation of drug use. For regular users, drugs stay in hair permanently or until the above is achieved. For this reason, hair is an excellent choice when rehabilitation monitoring is being conducted or risk positions are being offered to potential and existing employees.
- For a first-time user of drugs, we prefer to wait a week for the hair to grow the drug detection out from the scalp. This will then evidence the ingestion of the drug(s) which will have been deposited into the hair follicle via the blood stream.
- Body hair can be used but it has a less precise and wider window of detection than head hair. Body hair grows at a slower rate than head hair and can give an estimated window from 3 to 6 months or more.
- As a wide-window test medium, head or body hair has many more applications in the workplace than a narrow-window test medium.
- Hair analysis provides a wide-window examination of a person's use or non-use of substances. When considering testing people for substance misuse there is very large risk mitigation, such that if a donor has been

free from drugs for protracted periods of 90 days or more then they are more likely to remain free from substance misuse in the future.

What does wide-window testing bring to the table?

Consider the level of risk mitigation in the following workplace situations where there are safety or reputational questions to be considered, role-specific situations or application within the company's governance of substance and alcohol misuse. Some uses of hair testing are:

- Pre-employment
- Pre-promotion
- Rehabilitation
- Investigation
- Return to work, post-sickness
- Relocation or secondment to another site or company
- Support to narrow-window testing (used in tandem)
- Historical abuse pattern
- Prove and disprove claims of spiked drinks
- Prove false positives/negatives of narrow-window POC devices

Because hair is a wide-window test medium you cannot use hair on its own in a for-cause situation to determine recent use. It only provides an historical examination but can be used in tandem with a narrow-window test medium. Remember it takes approximately 1 week for the hair to grow long enough to detect a recent one-off drug use; regular drug use will be detected while the donor continues to use substances and alcohol. A wide-window test medium can, however, be used as part of the investigation in a for-cause situation, even where a fatality has occurred. I have often found that someone who has passed a POC instant test device or a BTL narrow-window test subsequently fails a wide-window test. So, always consider the tandem use of both in for-cause situations and other investigative applications.

Example

An incident occurs in the workplace where an injury has been sustained. With a narrow-window test medium time is a critical factor and the test should be conducted as soon as is practicable after the incident. You cannot use the narrow-window test if at the time the narrow-window of detection has already passed. Testing within minutes of the incident is critical, as it is no good when you leave it for 48 hours or more and then test. The incident has resulted in serious injury to one person but has involved five individuals in a chain reaction. All parties consent to being tested. When questioned one person admits to using drugs some 8 days prior. It is clear that narrow-window testing will not detect that usage time frame. What do you do?

The answer is, you still use a narrow-window test medium to see if the individual is telling the truth. Believe it or not, people lie with regard to their drug misuse. You also have the right to take the wide-window sample as long as it is allowed for in your policy. Your policy should state that an employee is required to be drug free at the time a request for a test is made. Because hair analysis is both quantitative and qualitative you can make a more considered judgement on the individual based on the toxicology report and the other evidence surrounding the cause of the incident.

Example

An employee was selected for a wide-window hair test and confessed that he had used cocaine while at a stag party in Europe. He further stated he had paid approximately £45 for a wrap of cocaine while drunk. The hair collection was still taken and analysed. The result was negative for any controlled substance whatsoever. The donor was not pleased when he received the result, which showed he had wasted £45 on a white powder that was not even a drug. There is no quality control or customer service complaint process in crime; you have to smile at situations like this, despite how serious they can become.

Where hair cannot be collected from the donor's head or body then *fingernail clippings* can be used, and they provide an approximate 6-month window of detection.

Hall & Angus, have created a workplace drug and alcohol testing brand called TOX247 Ltd. Our approach to workplace testing revolves around the following characteristics:

1. Rapid turnaround of BTL samples within 24 hours of receipt at the laboratory and the remainder within 48 hours.
2. The ability to test multiple drug groups in hair, including alcohol, anabolic steroids and stress (cortisol) in both saliva and hair.
3. A pre-analysis wash process to remove external contamination, when appropriate, including analysis of the wash if requested.

4. Price competitive per 7 to 9 drug group panel as well as additional individual compounds.
5. Expert witness support for analytical services and policy writing or workplace mediation services.

This workplace analytical service has been provided as a result of many years of commissioning other laboratories globally that failed to produce what we know to be achievable. Our collective goal is to have a turnaround of all UK BTL workplace samples within 24 hours of receipt at the laboratory. If your provider is taking longer than 48 hours, then you may want to review the on-cost with regard to full-pay suspension delays and other associated costs applied by the supplier or the inefficiency of your chosen POT. Your policy and other T&Cs of employment may also be severely tested at litigation.

Narrow-window testing

Narrow-window testing is used where the recent use of a substance needs to be identified or eliminated, e.g. when a for-cause incident has occurred. Narrow-window testing can be applied using different test mediums. Three in particular are

1. Saliva, time to collect = 5–10 minutes per donor including ChOC/ consent documentation, regardless of using BTL or a POC device.
2. Urine, time to prep a toilet = 15–30 minutes; time allowed for the donor to pass a sample = 3 hours or 1 hour before the end of a shift pattern, ChOC extra to the above. If there is no sample, defer to saliva as at 1.
3. Deep lung breath alcohol, time to collect = 2 minutes per donor, including consent documentation.

Note: Breath alcohol testing is also covered in Chapter 5. The difference between breath testing for alcohol and the use of urine or saliva for fixed panel drugs is that alcohol is a legal substance, illegal only under a set cut-off within the UK Road Traffic Act where a breath sample must be collected by a constable in uniform. See Chapter 3 for policy application of alcohol misuse in the workplace. What are the legal limits for breath alcohol in your country? What are the restrictions placed on law enforcement around the use of breath test devices in your country?

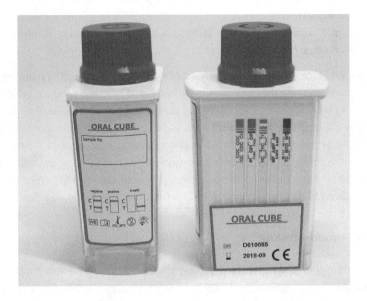

Figure 2.1 The picture above is an oral fluid (saliva) instant result screening device (courtesy of Martin Vickerman). These devices are non-evidential and are the start of a process to see if a donor is misusing any substances that are identified on the panel of drugs named. Many of these devices are looking for 40% of substances that are prescribed medications. Let's be clear there are no legal cut-offs for prescribed medications. The control for prescribed medications is the prescription. If the donor cannot provide a prescription, they will likely be breaking both criminal and civil legislations, and that is what should be applied in disciplinary action.

The remaining 60% of drugs are outright illegal substances but many are applied above a medicinal cut-off; e.g. cocaine is used in Novocaine for dental procedures, and other refined cocaine derivatives are used in prescribed medications. Opium when refined provides morphine for pain relief and is also used in many other medicinal compounds; the same is true of the majority of illegal drugs. Synthetic cannabis drugs and Ecstasy have no medicinal use and can therefore be managed as a gross misconduct under criminal activity. What is the policy in your country?

The instant test devices do not examine, nor can they examine for evidential purposes, cross-reactivity compounds or other metabolites that show substance misuse in the form of an illegal dose or illegal metabolite usage.

Like the breath test device, they are the start of a process in which a back to laboratory (BTL) collection device is submitted for evidential analysis within a validated process using mass spectrometry and examined by a reporting toxicologist. In addition, evidential analysis requires an A&B sample to be collected from the donor so that a challenge can be applied in law from another independent laboratory This cannot be provided from instant devices.

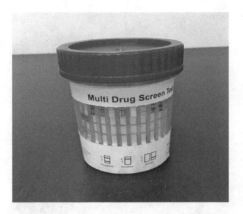

Figure 2.2 The picture above is an instant urine test device which has the same capability as the instant saliva device (courtesy of Martin Vickerman). The problem with urine is the need to have a controlled collection process and the application of countermeasures in the preparation of toilets, as well as a T&C time limit on the delivery of a urine sample, usually three hours.

The reagent strips showing two red lines indicate a negative sample. If the bottom line is not visible then the sample is considered a non-negative or presumptive positive and is subject to the same process as saliva and the collection of a BTL A&B sample.

The problem with the instant test devices is that, as mentioned previously, they are non-evidential and are the start of a process of looking for evidential value to be applied to T&Cs of employment and subsequently any disciplinary action. The only action that can be taken based on results from this device is suspension of the donor, usually on full pay, for a period by which your selected laboratory can respond with the result of a BTL sample submission. This can become very expensive for an initially cheap approach to workplace testing, especially if you are also paying for an independent collection agency.

The employer must consider seriously the on-cost these devices can generate.

You will see from Figure 2.2 that there are two red lines showing in every drug reagent strip. The top line shows a control line where sufficient fluid is present for analysis of the sample. If a lower red line is also visible then the sample is negative. If the bottom line is not visible at all then this is non-negative or presumptive positive for that drug group. The same is true of the instant saliva collection device.

Consider what you choose as your instant result test device, how it is applied and what action you take, especially in the following circumstances:

1. Pre-employment due diligence on short-term contracts.
2. Pre-employment as your preferred testing methodology; remember the device is non-evidential.
3. In disciplinary action, you cannot dismiss an employee based on the results from these devices alone.
4. When a prescription is produced for an opiate indication, there is no legal measure for prescribed medication limits, only an opinion from a GP.

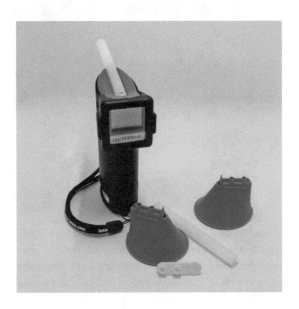

Figure 2.3 The picture above is an Intoximeter FST digital breath test device (courtesy of Intoximeter). This device examines deep lung breath for a concentration of alcohol per 100 millilitres of breath. The alcohol cut off can be set by the company but cannot exceed the country's drink driving limit. What is that limit in your country?

In the UK, roadside breath test devices are screening devices only and are *non-evidential*. For compliance with the UK drink driving regulations, the devices used by the police must have passed a home office specification to allow only a constable in uniform the power of arrest and detention in law, and only for the purpose of conducting, under the Road Traffic Act, the donor having an evidential test while in custody back at the police station. In the UK collection mechanisms are another evidential breath test machine and or blood or urine samples. These powers are not available in the workplace.

How should these screening devices be used in the workplace?

1. There is a need for an agreed figure to be set in an individual's terms and conditions (T&Cs) of employment.
2. The company must identify and notify all employees of that company limit and the consequences of breaching it within the T&Cs of employment.
3. The non-evidential breath test device is the start of a process which may, depending on circumstances and T&Cs of employment, lead to disciplinary action up to and including dismissal, if the T&Cs and policy so dictate.

In certain sectors the alcohol limit for certain professions is much lower; e.g., in aviation, flight and cabin crew, air traffic controllers and specified engineers, all have a maximum level of 9 micrograms of alcohol in 100 millilitres of breath. This limit is statutory to those professions and enforceable by law. Be very careful how you apply a screening device in your workplace. Ensure that what you are doing is legally defensible.

There are other narrow-window test mediums such as blood, which is an intimate sample and not generally collected for workplace situations. There is also sweat and residue swabbing but these have limited applications when compared against saliva and urine. Residue swabbing is useful when applied to an investigation or preparation of an investigation to identify drug misuse hot spots, such as toilets, stores, cabs of heavy goods vehicles, etc.

So, as far as narrow-window testing for substance misuse is concerned, what are the pros and cons between the use of saliva and urine in the workplace? We first concentrate on the 'evidential' BTL collection and submission of either test medium.

Pros of saliva testing

1. Saliva has the closest test window to blood, with most drug metabolites being detectable within 6 hours of ingestion and available for detection for up to 36 hours, possibly more depending on the purity of drug used and the regularity/amount used by the donor.
2. Saliva involves an easy collection method, with the donor being present throughout the collection and ChOC process.
3. The speed of collection of a saliva test is much quicker than for a urine sample, where the donor can deliberately or naturally fail/obstruct the passing of a sample of urine until their shift is over and then leave the site untested, go sick for a few days to abstain from substance misuse and come back to work to take a test they will then pass.
4. Saliva now has a quantifiable legal history of application similar to urine and in many cases is a better carrier of a drug metabolite.
5. Saliva can be easily collected in most locations whereas urine mostly requires access to a toilet facility.
6. Saliva is most appropriate for mass screening issues such as random testing programmes where companies require a percentage of the workforce or a shift pattern to be tested in a single visit.

Cons of saliva testing

1. In the event of dry mouth syndrome or a related medical condition, there may be a need to defer to urine.

Pros of urine testing

1. In the event of dry mouth syndrome or other related medical condition where saliva cannot be collected, urine is the alternative.

Cons of urine testing

1. With a urine sample, time has to be allowed for the donor(s) to provide a sample. In a policy this is usually within 3 hours of request or 1 hour before the end of a shift pattern.
2. During the delay period for the provision of a urine sample the donor has to be monitored and supervised. If the donor cannot subsequently provide a urine sample, then a saliva sample should be requested. Why not go that route in the first place?
3. In a UK workplace situation, the collection of a urine sample is unobserved when the donor is lost to view. This requires the application of other countermeasures to prevent adulteration of a urine sample.
4. In the UK there is a need to have access to toilet facilities for the provision of an unobserved urine collection and as such this requires that other countermeasures are taken, such as
   - Isolating other toilet cubicles
   - Searching the toilets for hidden masking agents and equipment used to beat urine testing, methodologies that are widely available on the internet
   - Searching the donor for hidden masking agents and equipment, including drug-free urine of another person or bought over the internet
   - Consideration to closing off the water supply to all areas within the toilet
   - Addition of loo-blue or other agent into the toilet u-bend(s)
   - Examination of the creatinine levels in the urine sample to prove it is human urine
   - Examination of the pH level of the urine for dilution, deliberate or otherwise
   - Examination of the temperature of the urine to show that it has come directly from the body as opposed to another delivery mechanism
5. As a result of the above, urine is not appropriate for mass screening programmes.

From the above you may see why at Hall & Angus (TOX247) we recommend the use of hair analysis combined with saliva for a robust workplace Programme of Testing and the application of wide- and narrow-window test mediums, independently of each other or in tandem.

POC testing or BTL testing

The weakness of POC (instant result screening devices) is that it is **'non-evidential'** and cannot be used to dismiss an employee, only to suspend them on full pay while the BTL process is activated. BTL analysis is evidential/confirmatory testing and does not always require suspension until the result is received and affirmative action can be taken against the donor on production of a toxicologist's report.

I accept the need for both methods but do not agree with the amount of UK POC testing that is being conducted as the primary methodology of detecting/preventing substance misuse in the workplace. There are many reports that state POC collection devices provide false-positive or false-negative results. This is an issue with regard to employment law, so let's identify some more issues.

POC devices in the UK

1. POC devices are non-evidential when used on existing employees.
2. POC devices are screening devices only, which may or may not detect drugs from a limited panel of drugs and are not generally trusted
3. POC devices have a fixed panel of drugs that unless bought in bulk are not changed.
4. POC devices only detect a presumptive positive and therefore the only affirmative action that can be taken from such a result is the full-pay suspension of the donor and the move to a BTL collection device and process. This then puts the pressure on your laboratory provider to complete a rapid BTL response. How long does your provider take on BTL results? When compared with the testing process, what is the daily pay rate of suspending an employee on full pay for up to 10 days, with some UK providers?
5. The donor cannot be dismissed on the POC result or have any other affirmative action taken against them, except full-pay suspension.

6. The mistrust around the instant devices dilutes the robust nature of a company POT with a process which is costly and humiliating when a BTL analysis provides a negative, evidential result.

7. There are very few workplace situations where a POC device is preferable to a rapid BTL device.

8. At contractor induction programmes POC devices are being used to exclude some contract employees from work, even on production of a prescription for opiate-positive indications. I would like to see that approach challenged in court and would be happy to respond as an expert witness.

9. A previous large UK employer was using POC devices and presumptive positive results to ban contractors from their operations for life. I would also like to see that challenged in court as at 8.

The above situations apply to full-time or part-time staff/contracts. What is the situation in your country with regard to this approach? The following applies or is applied when used as a pre-employment device:

1. Some companies will apply POC testing prior to employment and use the devices to decline employment permanently.

2. Proof of medication is required when an opiate indication is provided as a presumptive positive. *A large number of potential employees have been discovered who are using their partner's or another's prescription opiates to self-medicate using a Class B drug off prescription. Employer response: Zero Tolerance.*

3. Some companies still decline employment when a prescription is provided to evidence an opiate presumptive positive result.

4. Specific POC devices are used with specific compounds within healthcare and continuous prescribing protocols. These are not generally used in the workplace, unless part of an employee's rehabilitation process.

Chain of custody

Chain of custody (ChOC) is the term given to the legal requirements of collecting and packaging the donor's sample for shipping to a regulated/accredited laboratory. In the UK that is a UKAS 17025 accreditation. At the laboratory an initial inspection will be conducted to make sure the sample packaging is intact and has not been tampered with, all tamper-proof seals are intact and above all, the consents and identities have been achieved and signed for.

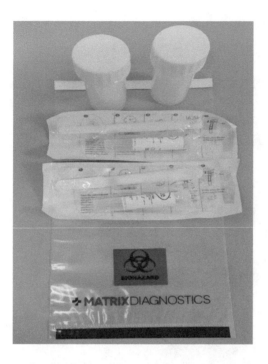

Figure 2.4 The picture above is a back to laboratory (BTL) oral fluid (saliva) package (courtesy of Matrix Diagnostics). Note: there are two sealed saliva collection devices, two transportation tubes an evidence bag with indestructible seal. Many labs also provide their own specific sample collection documents as well as pre- paid postage envelopes.

Once a BTL sample is taken under the chain of custody (ChOC) and all packing and collection paperwork is completed, the sample can be sent to the laboratory. Remember that use of all test devices, whether instant or BTL, requires a signed document of consent by the donor.

Unlike the instant saliva test, the BTL device is evidential and provides for two samples (A&B), one of which will be analysed by the company's selected and accredited laboratory. In the event the first sample is analysed as positive the second sample will be kept and provided to the donor for independent analysis if the result is contested by the donor. The holding laboratory will be responsible for shipping the B sample to the donor's chosen laboratory.

The first result, positive or negative, is reported back to the designated company representative. In the UK the second sample is frozen for up to 7 years before it is discarded. What is the duration of sample retention in your country?

The controls and extra degree of toxicological analysis are the basis for the legality of the analytical process. Samples would fail the whole process if the ChOC has not been met, or the sample had fatal flaws on BTL examination. With a narrow test window, the window for detection is lost if the sample is rejected or lost. There is a need with all narrow-window sample processes, such as for saliva and urine, to have a wide option available, such as hair or fingernail clippings. See Hair collection section.

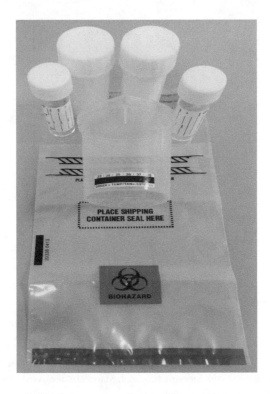

Figure 2.5 The picture above shows a traditional back to laboratory (BTL) collection package for urine. Again you can see two sample collection devices as per the saliva BTL unit. This again allows for an A&B sample provision and subsequent challenge by the donor to your selected laboratory toxicology report. The collection cup, like the instant urine device, shows a temperature strip to show the fluid collected is at body temperature. There is a need to have countermeasures in place to detect masking agents / processes with urine collection.

As with the saliva BTL collection device different laboratories also provide different sample collection forms and pre-paid packaging envelopes.

Different countries have different collection and postal procedures for what is a BIOHAZARD fluid. Be sure you understand what those shipping regulations are.

Again, with any sample collection there is a need for documented proof of consent with any testing process, whether BTL or screening.

Urine is a narrow-window test medium, although cannabis can be detected in urine for up to approximately 28 days, depending on strength and regularity of use by the donor.

As urine comes through different organs in the body than saliva, you cannot compare the results of a urine test against one for saliva or hair. All test medium results have to be considered separately and their own characteristics taken into account.

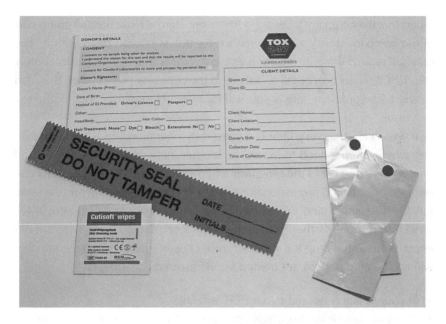

Figure 2.6 The picture above shows a hair and fingernail collection kit. Both mediums are wide-window test mediums. Cut head hair is approximately one month of history for each centimetre of hair. For equality reasons cut head hair is generally restricted to 3 centimetres across all genders. Body hair can show 6 months' history, as can fingernail clippings.

Wide-window *testing* has many more applications than narrow-window testing.

Cut head hair can also be segmented for investigation purposes of spiked drinks defences or regular/habitual use rehabilitation countermeasures applied to the company Employee Assistance Programme.

The best methodology to manage workplace substance misuse management is to stop the substance misuser from getting into the workplace in the first instance. Where people can abstain for short periods to beat a narrow-window prescheduled test (saliva-urine), they cannot abstain for the 90 days applied to a hair sample.

In-house training of suitable employees to collect samples and complete a full ChOC protocol is preferable and is the most cost-effective and efficient way to conduct workplace testing. These employees are called Designated Employee Representatives (DERs). It is often argued that it is preferable for sample collection to be an independent situation, which is a strange idea that increases the cost of the sample process ten-fold. The only part of the testing process that is independent is the laboratory analysis. It is on the basis of that report that the company takes any subsequent affirmative action; all else is part of the company policy and governance regardless of who deals with it. The only fallback of using an independent collector is that if they fail to comply with ChOC collection or fail to adhere to the company process then they can be sued. The problem here is you will have likely lost all evidence of the test as a result.

If we accept that very little is achieved by operational POC random testing, why is there a need to introduce another ineffective, time delaying and unnecessary on-cost to the programme? Properly trained company DERs can respond quickly and professionally to any workplace substance misuse issue, just like first aiders and fire marshalls. Do you call an ambulance or a fire service to respond to these situations in the workplace? *No*, so why is it different for a simple drug test process? Your chosen substance misuse supplier will ensure all situations are trained for. Be assured:

- If your policy is not right your POT will fail.
- A minor failure of the ChOC process will require remedial action but your sample can be analysed, as long as the minor failure is reported and accounted for, even to the point of an affidavit.
- If your ChOC is fatally flawed your sample will fail inspection and will not be analysed and there will be no toxicology reporting.
- For wide-window test mediums you can simply take another sample and get the ChOC process correct.
- In narrow-window testing the window of detection is often lost and therefore the evidence is lost. Because of the rate of growth of hair you can wait a week to engage the wide-window process when a narrow-window sample is lost, for whatever reason. Your policy must reflect this countermeasure.

Toxicology reporting

Confirmatory toxicology from your analytical provider will report on:

1. A positive result for a controlled/other substance.
2. A negative result for a list of identified drug groups or compounds.
3. Trace detection of a compound but below cut-off. *This is the type of report that needs careful consideration, as the trace below cut-off is always a negative scenario. It is useful, however, in employee rehabilitation and some investigative situations, such as a low positive detection of cocaine but a below cut-off detection of benzoylecgonine, found in illicit cocaine.*

Figure 2.7 shows a sample toxicology report from our partners at Cansford Laboratories. Use this type of reporting as your minimum requirement. You will see from the Cansford report that it contains the following information:

- A list of compounds; other cross-reactivity compounds are added as and when detected, e.g. cocaethylene, found when illicit cocaine is used in tandem with alcohol.
- A list of cut-offs, which is essential when considering the rehabilitation or removal of an employee from within the company. The amount by which a donor is above cut-off is a pointer towards an occasional, regular or chaotic misuse management scenario. Some laboratories will not give you any report other than positive, which is not acceptable when considering a person's future if the person may have self-referred or you as an employer actually want to keep them despite the substance misuse issues, which now have to be managed.
- The signature of the toxicology reporting officer.
- The date the sample was collected.
- The date the sample arrived at the laboratory.
- The date the sample was analysed and reported back to the client.
- The donor's details (optional but with another, covert identifier such as payroll number, national insurance number, etc.).
- The collection officer's details, essential if repeat collection issues arise that may require further training of the collector.
- The company code; in the event of a third-party provider there is a need for that third party to know which of their clients the report applies to.

On receipt of this toxicology report Hall & Angus will work with our clients by providing our opinion of the content relevant to the applied test situation, such as:

- If it is a positive pre-employment zero-tolerance test, the employment application is rejected for at least 6 months.
- If it is a for-cause test the toxicology report is significant to any affirmative action taken.
- If it is a rehabilitation test the employer's response will be considered around the T&Cs of employment and the conditions of the EAP; see Chapter 5.

LABORATORIES
For decisions that really matter

LABORATORIES

Cansford Laboratories Limited
1a Pentwyn Business Centre
Wharfedale Road, Cardiff, CF23 7HB
Tel: 029 20540567 (Alt: 033 033 27979)
info@cansfordlabs.co.uk

Certificate of Analysis
All analysis performed by Cansford Laboratories

Name:	Mr Anon	Total hair length:	cm	Client:	Mr Anon (MR0020)
DOB:	08-Jan-1935	Hair colour:	Black		Some Street
Gender:	M	Hair site:	Head		
Sample pack:	ABarCode	Date received:	17-May-2018		A Town
Collection date:	16-May-2018	Case Ref:			Post code: AA01 AAA

Section ID:	100400		Section Length from-to (cm): 0-3	
Period:	Approximately from 09-Feb-2018 to 10-May-2018		Analysis: Started -	Completed - 17-May-2018

Amphetamine (Method LC-MS/MS)	Result	(Cut-off)
† Amphetamine	0.3 ng/mg	(0.2ng/mg)

Benzodiazepines (Method LC-MS/MS)	Result	(Cut-off)
† 7-Aminoclonazepam	Not detected	(0.03ng/mg)
† Alprazolam	Not detected	(0.03ng/mg)
† Bromazepam	Not detected	(0.03ng/mg)
† Chlordiazepoxide	Not detected	(0.1ng/mg)
† Clonazepam	Not detected	(0.03ng/mg)
† Diazepam	Not detected	(0.03ng/mg)
† Lorazepam	Not detected	(0.03ng/mg)
† Midazolam	Not detected	(0.03ng/mg)
† Nitrazepam	Not detected	(0.03ng/mg)
† Nordiazepam	Not detected	(0.03ng/mg)
† Oxazepam	Not detected	(0.03ng/mg)
† Temazepam	Not detected	(0.03ng/mg)

Cannabinoids (Method LC-MS/MS)	Result	(Cut-off)
† 11-Nor-delta9-THC-carboxylic Acid	Not detected	(0.0003ng/mg)
† Cannabidiol	Not detected	(0.02ng/mg)
† Cannabinol	Not detected	(0.02ng/mg)
† delta9-tetrahydrocannabinol (THC)	Not detected	(0.02ng/mg)

Cocaine (Method LC-MS/MS)	Result	(Cut-off)
† Anhydroecgonine methyl ester	0.2 ng/mg	(0.1ng/mg)
† Benzoylecgonine	0.15 ng/mg	(0.05ng/mg)
† Cocaethylene	0.15 ng/mg	(0.05ng/mg)
† Cocaine	0.6 ng/mg	(0.5ng/mg)
† Norcocaine	Not detected	(0.05ng/mg)

Methadone (Method LC-MS/MS)	Result	(Cut-off)
† EDDP	Not detected	(0.02ng/mg)
† Methadone	Not detected	(0.2ng/mg)

Methamphetamines & Ecstasy (Method LC-MS/MS)	Result	(Cut-off)
† MBDB (Methylenedioxyphenyl-2-butanamine)	Not detected	(0.2ng/mg)
† MDA (Methylenedioxyamphetamine)	Not detected	(0.2ng/mg)
† MDEA (Methylenedioxyethylamphetamine)	Not detected	(0.2ng/mg)
† MDMA (Methylenedioxymethylamphetamine)	Not detected	(0.2ng/mg)
† Methamphetamine	Not detected	(0.2ng/mg)

Opiates (Method LC-MS/MS)	Result	(Cut-off)
† 6-Acetylcodeine	Not detected	(0.2ng/mg)
† 6-Acetylmorphine	Not detected	(0.2ng/mg)
† Codeine	Not detected	(0.2ng/mg)
† Diacetylmorphine (Heroin)	Not detected	(0.2ng/mg)
† Dihydrocodeine	Not detected	(0.2ng/mg)
† Morphine	0.3 ng/mg	(0.2ng/mg)

Figure 2.7 Sample toxicology report.

How do some employees/job applicants respond to a workplace POT and SAMP?

Of course, there is the other aspect of workplace substance misuse countermeasures, which are the obstruction steps taken by employees or pre-employment applicants. Methods to beat a drug test are widely available/

claimed on the internet and dark web. There is a multimillion-pound business that revolves around countermeasures for sale to help an employee or applicant beat the workplace test using a masking agent, the vast majority of which do not work.

Websites that advertise masking agents or fake diversion kits receive more hits per month than service providers looking to eradicate this problem from the workplace and society. Training your workplace representatives in the key areas of the SAMP, POT and EAP is critical and needs your input to achieve a safe working environment and compliance with civil and criminal legislations.

The following is for your consideration in the UK:

- Managers should be trained to deal with workers who seek help. (ACAS)
- Unions strongly believe that there is no place for drugs in the workplace. Any person who is under the influence of drugs while working can be a danger to both the worker and their colleagues. Where drugs are used in the workplace it is often to combat either fatigue or stress. These should be addressed by removing the cause of the problem. In either situation a person will have a physical addiction to a substance – in which case they need help to address this. (TUC Guidance on Drug Testing in the Workplace, May 2010)
- Thirty-eight per cent of drug users with a psychiatric disorder were receiving no treatment at all. (Drug Scope)
- Poor mental health costs UK employers £8.4 billion on average every year in absence due to sickness and £15.1 billion in reduced productivity. (ACAS)
- Alcohol and drug policies should be used to ensure problems are dealt with effectively and consistently. (ACAS)
- There is a need for employers to have a robust substance and alcohol policy and a structured approach to an employee assistance programme. (BMA)

Chapter summary

At Hall & Angus Ltd. we firmly believe in the rapid turnaround of BTL samples. We also firmly believe in the predominant use of wide- and narrow-window test mediums used under the right circumstances and for the right reasons. We are firm believers in the predominant and proven use of BTL testing as opposed to POC testing. This chapter has outlined years of experience of testing methodologies across numerous situations in commerce and industry globally.

Hopefully, this chapter will provide you with the right information to set those SLAs of your own, apply KPIs of your own, but most importantly help you get value for money now that you know how test mediums work and what sample turnaround times can be achieved. It makes no difference who your preferred provider is; it is your SAMP, it is your POT, it is your EAP and it is your T&Cs of employment that are being applied within your business. If the provider of the workplace substance misuse countermeasures cannot meet your standards, there are providers that can.

The following are some do's and do not's. As you will have your own list, these are provided to stimulate your thought process and help you select what you do want and do not want.

Do

1. Consider what each test medium can and cannot do.
2. Consider the fact you need both narrow- and wide-window test mediums under a wide range of situations.
3. Consider how you will set your SLAs and KPIs with your substance and alcohol misuse analytical provider(s).
4. Choose your analytical services carefully, check their accreditations and consider their turnaround times. Are you happy with their costs, and can you eliminate unnecessary on-cost imposed by your supplier's inefficiencies?
5. Consider substance and alcohol misuse management as part of the company investigative toolbox and the up-skilling of your management team.
6. Consider training and communication in the awareness of test mediums and how they integrate into your company before they are imposed for a variety of reasons.
7. Consider the need to understand drug metabolites and cross-reactivity compounds; they are also an essential part of management training.
8. Conduct competitive tendering for your requirements around workplace substance misuse countermeasures.

9. Rely on BTL testing for evidence in the decision-making process of the dismissal/retention of any employee.
10. Make sure your laboratory reports how much over a cut-off the employee's sample analysis is. It is essential in how you rehabilitate them or make a decision as to their being not fit for purpose.
11. Make sure your sample turnaround times are not the cause of a significant on-cost and employee absence for no reason.

Do not

1. Ignore the need to have testing in your employee and pre-employment management strategies.
2. Forget that if an employee in the UK self-refers, you need a structured methodology to legally assess and manage their recovery or removal from the business. *What is the situation in your country?*
3. Develop your substance misuse programme around an inappropriate test medium which has limitations that restrict your substance misuse management strategy.
4. Dismiss staff on the basis of POC/instant test device results. They are not evidential but rather are screening devices in the UK. *What are they in your country?*
5. Dismiss staff on the basis of a breath alcohol test device result. These are not evidential but rather are screening devices in the UK. *What are they in your country?*
6. Rely on a weak SAMP and POT to justify or support the dismissal of staff using any screening device.
7. Think that by simply having a random testing programme you have a strong deterrent. You do not. You need a robust policy and a robust Programme of Testing, *which is your best deterrent.*

Substance and alcohol misuse policy

Writing, development and implementation

Introduction

Chapters 1 and 2 provided you with a basic examination of people and drugs and test mediums. The meaning of the phrase basic examination is now changed in this chapter, which is designed to give you the *very best start* for what a company Substance and Alcohol Misuse Policy (SAMP) should look like, many of the considerations and a format unique to Hall & Angus.

At Hall & Angus we have designed a four-phase modular structure that we then bespoke to client needs, which may be driven by sector as well as role-specific legislations. We also use this structure when we provide a review of a client's or potential client's existing policy. We *will not* work with a client whose policy or Programme of Testing (POT) is not legal and robust or does not meet our minimum standards.

SAMP writing is a skill I have developed over years of experience, nationally and internationally. It also encompasses a variety of negative experiences gathered from other disciplines that have tried but had no formal training in writing a SAMP, POT or Employee Assistance Programme (EAP), such as health & safety, human resources, law, occupational health and so on. Members of trade unions who very often represent their members at disciplinary hearings go through a two-year diploma programme without any training with regard to workplace substance misuse or countermeasures. Is there any wonder that conflict exists between individuals who do not know the subject but have to apply employment law and criminal and civil legislations to terms and conditions (T&Cs) of employment around what is a very complicated subject?

Until the evolution of Hall & Angus Ltd there were no formal accredited training courses for the writing of a SAMP in the UK, especially what we consider a comprehensive and defensible SAMP. With that in mind, there was also no formal training for those who pontificate within criminal or civil judiciary with regard to the SAMP and its correlation to the POT and EAP that is so important in the building of a robust programme allied to toxicology and other relevant processes.

In the early days of examining this situation, approaches were made to a variety of membership organizations such as the UK Chartered Institute of Personnel & Development (CIPD), Health Safety executives, trade unions, universities and many more. None were prepared to offer the training or pay for it to be delivered as an accreditation of up-skilling/education for those individuals charged with the management of such an important subject that massively impacts employees' lives, all 35 million of them in the UK. *How many employees operate within your country's working population?* The consequences of employers getting the substance and alcohol misuse policy wrong and applying it to the detriment of the company and the employee can have far-reaching and devastating fiscal or life-changing ramifications that are in fact easily avoidable. The Hall &Angus Continuing Professional Development (CPD) accredited courses were therefore developed from our business support remit in 2016 and are very much part of this book.

A great many people or companies mentioned, surely solicitors, HR departments, health & safety and occupational health provide those substance misuse services. Let me tell you, I have had access to and viewed hundreds of SAMPs, many developed by each of these providers, and none have been fit for purpose. Most have been biased towards their own service provision or profession, and some have actually been illegal in the supporting advice they provide. This is especially true of employer and employee membership organizations that feel they need to provide the substance and alcohol misuse advice service but have not properly resourced who the experts actually are in the subject or the wide range of workplace substance and alcohol misuse countermeasures that need consideration within a wide variety of support and investigative mechanisms.

Many policies are downloaded from dubious internet providers who have not had their policies examined via litigation or to bespoke specific situations. All contain non-enforceable woffle commonly known as general information, not policy. More importantly, if the SAMP is not properly built around an effective and firm POT and EAP, which is critical to a robust and defensible workplace package that deals *effectively and consistently* with workplace substance and alcohol misuse.

In the process of responding to numerous companies' requests for support on the SAMP and subsequent action taken against employees, we found it alarming that the advice given by other types of employer and employee memberships, especially when they openly admit they have very little expertise in the subject, do not believe in the subject but have advised dismissal of employees for all the wrong reasons.

If the vast majority of employees had better knowledge of their rights, they would be better positioned to challenge their dismissal in most cases, and very likely win. In the case of employers, they would be better positioned to prevent workplace confrontation caused by making the wrong decision but also better positioned to provide employees with the confidence that their company knows what it is doing. The fact is, there are too many organizations that claim to be experts on the subject of workplace substance and alcohol misuse management when in fact they are very far from that capability.

'The Substance and Alcohol Misuse Policy (SAMP) is exactly the same for a company with 10 staff or 100,000 staff. The laws and processes around the litigating of one person are exactly the same for everyone regardless of the size of company in which they work within a SAMP.'

– Trevor Hall

This chapter and its considered content are dedicated to those professionals who are charged with writing and implementing a policy, managing the process and building the POT and EAP that protects the company while treating its potential and existing employees with dignity. It will also help educate those employees who have fallen foul of a poor policy or POT that has impacted their current or potential employability, and in the process has humiliated them.

The need to know or understand

The development and implementation of a robust and legally defensible companywide SAMP, POT and EAP embedded into T&Cs of employment requires knowledge of and at the very least consideration of the following subjects:

1. **Knowledge of relevant civil and criminal laws.** There are a variety of legislations that are applied within and away from the workplace. Some are identified in this book, and there are a great many that are country specific. Be sure you have been advised properly as to how to apply them and examine the culpabilities of company directors balanced against the responsibilities of others, which is the true role of the solicitor/ compliance officer in this process. It is my opinion that putting acts and sections of legislations into policy documents is very bad practice. You cannot put all relevant legislations into the policy and those you leave out will be equally as important to the protection of the company and the management of its employees. You may also find yourself defending intricacies of those acts that are continually argued in courts of all levels in all countries and in case-stated debate. The great many criminal and civil legislations that can be applied to the workplace point towards the SAMP and POT being more of a compulsory provision than a voluntary option.

2. **Knowledge of statutory requirements.** Every country has a list of statutory requirements that will impact certain policies, T&Cs of employment and even questions that should be asked at pre-employment interviews. At Hall & Angus we have identified those that have an impact on workplace substance and alcohol misuse policies as well as T&Cs of employment in the UK. Make sure you know what they are for your country and that where necessary they become part of your Standard Operating Procedures (SOPs). You may find you are complicit in committing the same offence as your employee if you fail to take note and they disregard your policies or enhanced induction strategies. Induction protocols around the SAMP, POT and EAP are the starting place for the need to conduct more certificated awareness training during an employee's term of employment.

'Better training will lead to less of a need for poor testing protocols that are expensive, negatively impact business efficiency and most of all discredit the whole programme'

– Trevor Hall

85

3. **Knowledge of relevant employment laws.** Employment laws vary from country to country and sector to sector, regardless of which country/company the SAMP, POT or EAP is being applied to. Substance and alcohol misuse has ramifications within civil and criminal legislations globally. There is a need to identify what are the best procedures to be applied to the company's approach to relevant employment law. In most cases, with regard to substance and alcohol misuse, the science is irrefutable; it's the procedures employed by the company that fail closer scrutiny. Interpretation and application of employment law need to be applied within the structure of the SAMP and the application of the POT and EAP. Solicitors need to embrace this approach and seek expert support/ training.

4. **Knowledge of terms and conditions of employment.** Knowledge of T&Cs of employment follows on from 1, 2 and 3. If each of the first three items have been properly considered the T&Cs should be a natural progression with regard to a robust and effective SAMP, POT and EAP. There will be a steady stream of legislations which will come along from time to time and require that T&Cs of employment undergo constant monitoring; by the same token this is also true of the SAMP, POT and EAP. Be sure that your employees are aware not only of their contractual agreement through a robust and documented induction protocol, but also of their requirement to comply with the law of the land in which they are operating and/or living.

5. **Knowledge of test mediums and collection protocols.** Knowledge of what a test medium can and cannot do is imperative. The SAMP is not the POT. The SAMP is a set of standards which when breached have a range of consequences that are agreed on within a specific company that has applied due consideration to the company- or sector-specific requirements. The POT is the analytical processes applied in conjunction with the circumstances outlined in the SAMP and applied to those identified in the SAMP. The donors' sample collection and laboratory submission protocols will require a set of SOPs to ensure the *chain of custody* of the collection is not compromised. Each test medium used will have its own characteristics, and the metabolite *cut-offs* from one test medium cannot be compared with those of other test mediums. You cannot compare the characteristics of urine with those of hair or saliva and likewise between them all. A fuller explanation of test mediums can be found in Chapter 2.

6. **Knowledge of sample chain of custody protocols.** Chain of custody (ChOC) is that process applied to the test medium collection, record taking and packaging by a range of regulatory requirements and the need for a sample to arrive at an analytical laboratory undamaged and not tampered with during or after collection. It will make no difference if a sample is suspected to be positive; if the chain of custody is compromised so is the chance of the sample being examined. If the fault is minor this can be overcome with an affidavit from the collector or person who may have missed a simple requirement. Fatal submission occurs if the sample has been tampered with or significant failings have occurred in any part of the collection and delivery process. Remember that the collection of any sample has to be with the written and recorded consent of the donor. The donor should be managed with dignity and professionalism throughout the whole collection and chain of custody process. The SAMP will need to reflect a refusal or obstruction of the collection of a sample.

7. **Knowledge of personal misuse of substance and alcohol issues.** Different drugs affect people in a variety of ways. An individual's route to substance misuse or dependency can be very complicated and there is a need in any self-referral situation to understand the donor's treatment history and identification of any unmet needs. A treatment profile and ultimately a treatment outcome needs to be developed specific to the donor's individual circumstances. These are the basic requirements of managing a person's misuse issues within a workplace EAP (see Chapter 4). There are of course other factors such as the donor's mental and physical wellbeing. Substance and alcohol misuse /dependency brings with it a range of other co-morbidities that also need to be taken into consideration during the management of that individual. The workplace situation requires a different approach to long-term interventions. In the UK the overriding factor is: An employee has a 'Fiduciary duty to be fit for work'. *What is this factor in your country? How do you manage it within T&Cs of employment? Where is it recorded?*

8. **Knowledge of existing company policies and protocols.** A company will have a variety of policies to be applied to its operations and its employees on and away from company premises. Many can and do cross over; for example, the use of a company vehicle will require some statutory requirements to be complied with, especially around drink and drug driving, the use of company phones while driving and more. The operation of heavy and light machinery will have SOPs to be complied with. All

are dependent on the employee being fit for duty or fit and authorized to operate a particular piece of equipment and so on. It's one thing to have a policy to switch off lights when an office is not in use and another where a legal requirement can be applied to the company and its officers under a variety of civil and criminal legislations. It's this very area which in my opinion makes the SAMP, POT and EAP more of a compulsory than a voluntary requirement, and there are culpabilities in law for those who do not deal properly with this *hidden threat within any workplace.*

9. **Knowledge of criminality surrounding substance misuse.** The misuse of illegal substances; the misuse of prescribed legal substances off prescription (including black market); and the variety of offences of possession, use, trafficking, manufacturing or being impaired by such substances have a wide variety of signs and symptoms, as well as culpabilities. In the UK many legally prescribed medications are actually controlled substances, Class A, B or C, under the Misuse of Drugs Act. The relevant powers of arrest and prosecution can be applied; e.g. tramadol, off prescription, is a Class C drug in the UK. The control is the prescription; the person who supplies the tramadol, whether they have a prescription or not, is dealing in a Class C drug and the person receiving it is in possession of a Class C drug. The relevant penalties for possession and supply can be, but rarely are, applied to both parties. The penalties for possession/trafficking, importing and exporting controlled substances vary from country to country. Some penalties are punitive, and others can carry the death sentence. In the UK, if an employer knowingly allows the dealing and possession of a Class A, B or C drug on their premises, then they also commit a criminal offence. *What is the situation in your country?* There are a great many criminality situations around the issues of misuse of substances in the workplace with regard to illegal and legal substances. *Who is protecting the employer and the employee from them? Do you trust the advice you have been given by a so-called expert?*

10. **General Data Protection Regulation (GDPR).** In the UK and EU the Data Protection Act (DPA) is applied to protect any information held by an organization about an individual. With regard to substance and alcohol misuse, the treatment or referral of the employee's issues must include the confidential records of that person's management or treatment of their individual situation. Accordingly, the DPA and GDPR need to be taken seriously, especially when it comes to self-referral issues and the handling of toxicology reporting or clinical interventions. The UK/EU

GDPR has applied controls in addition to those contained in the Data Protection Act. Companies will have to apply GDPR to any company SAMP, POT and EAP and to the manner by which they train and apply consent to employees. Consent in the UK and EU can no longer be a perception or expectation because of policy or tradition; there has to be a written acknowledgement of that consent at every stage of the need to take a course of action. Be aware that the penalties for not complying with the UK/EU's GDPR can be quite severe, up to 4% of annual turnover. There are issues outlined in this book that help manage DPA/GDPR and their ramifications by the correct development of T&Cs, releases from liability, training, consent and how it is achieved/recorded, as well as disclaimers necessary for compliance within a SAMP, POT and EAP. *What are the regulations in your country?* For the UK visit www.ico.org. uk. *Where can you research your country's guidelines? How will you apply them to your policy-building process?*

11. **Knowledge of toxicology reporting.** Toxicology reporting varies between analytical laboratories. I have seen some very poor and some very good reporting protocols. There is a need to identify in any Service Level Agreement (SLA) exactly what it is you need from your analytical laboratory and any subsequent toxicology report. The following comprise the bare minimum:

  • The type of drug/drug metabolite or cross-reactivity compound being looked for in the panel of drugs, agreed by you with your provider and subsequently discovered during analysis.
  • The legal cut-off for each drug across the panel, whether a clinical or another standard of workplace cut-off is applied.
  • The volume of drug metabolite or cross-reactivity compound found in the sample that is above the agreed cut-off for the situation it is being applied to.
  • An opinion if the analysis by drug group, drug metabolite or cross-reactive compound is positive or negative.
  • An identified signature of a reporting officer.
  • Above all, a rapid response turnaround of properly reported samples.

Remember, this information has to be accurate, as you will be deciding the future of an individual's continued employment or the level of employee assistance that can be provided. The amount of drug found will help look at whether the user has an occasional or chronic misuse problem, and this will help you decide on the nature of any rehabilitation or disciplinary action. It can also be a red flag to work-place drug use, trafficking situations and the safeguarding guidelines for the donor's family situation (if any) for the UK. *What are the safe-guarding guidelines in your country and what statutory requirements are applied to them/you?*

12. **Knowledge of drug metabolites and cross-reactivity compounds.** Drug metabolites and cross-reactive compounds are crucial when toxicologists are looking for specific markers. For example, cocaine is used in a variety of medications, and refined medicinal cocaine will have a medicinal cut-off for the toxicology report. It is completely feasible that a person can be misusing prescribed medications far above the medicinal cut-off or via black market activity or purchase from the so-called dark web. What we are also looking for is the metabolite of illicit cocaine, which is ben-zoylecgonine. Another cross-reactivity compound of cocaine is coca-ethylene, often found when illicit cocaine has been used simultaneously with alcohol. There are similar situations with heroin, amphetamine and many other illegal substances and the vast majority of compounds/metabolites. Point of care (POC), instant test devices cannot get to some of these metabolites/cross-reactive compounds and can only go after the drug group, e.g. opiates, which includes medicinal applications such as co-codamol, codeine and so on. Amphetamines and methamphetamines may have cutting agents such as ephedrine, a chest decongestant. Codeine is the base drug for making desomorphine, commonly known by the street name krokodil. The knowledge of metabolites and cross-reactivity compounds is a very complicated subject, especially when applying the consequences of use/possession to an individual's future. You need to rely on a reputable service provider/investigator and ensure that you are being properly advised on this very complicated subject which has to be situated within a variety of workplace countermeasures, such as the SAMP, POT and EAP; the company disciplinary procedure; corporate governance; and so on.

13. **Knowledge of the company's discipline procedures.** The disciplinary procedure is the end game of affirmative action with regard to substance and alcohol misuse or where criminal offences are also being committed. It makes no difference what action is to be taken or in which set of circumstances; there is a need to cover them all in a policy either by direct reference or possibly within a range of countermeasures such as: 'Disciplinary action will be taken up to and including dismissal.' It's only

fair to the individual that they already know the severity of the company's approach on such matters. Remember, in the UK, you cannot dismiss an employee who self-refers a substance or alcohol dependency or misuse issue; you have to manage them. *What is the situation in your country?* To manage them you need an EAP that has exclusion, enrolment and removal criteria.

See Chapter 4 on the Employee Assistance Programme (EAP).

14. **Knowledge of the company's governance of health & safety protocols.** Health Safety within a company is covered under a variety of legislations, regardless of country. Failure to comply with these regulations has ramifications. A company can have as many health & safety policies, SOPs and applications as it likes but all have to be overridden by a simple consideration/question: *Is or was the employee fit for work at the time they arrived at and during work?* The examination of training given, cognitive abilities, compliance with SOPs, etc. are the starting point of any investigation into fatality, injury, damage, culpability and responsibility. How the incident happened is usually obvious, and other issues require proof, either beyond all reasonable doubt or in the balance of probability depending on which court any situation is being or could be presented to. SAMPs, POTs and EAPs are introduced under health & safety but are managed and administered by HR. The application of a comprehensive and robust SAMP, POT and EAP is a provision to protect the company, its officers and its employees. The SAMP and POT also have a part to play in how a company sets the standards for contractors to comply with. *Are you in control of your company/department and those who work within it with regard to substance and alcohol misuse?*

15. **Knowledge of pre-employment/recruitment protocols.** A wide-window test medium (hair analysis) is essential in pre-employment and recruitment protocols. Studies have shown that there is a significant and quantifiable on-cost to an employer per year, per misuser employed. Some of the reasons for this are that substance and alcohol misusers have been shown to:
    - Have increased accident rates.
    - Have increased absenteeism.
    - Require higher agency or overtime costs to cover absenteeism.
    - Have had multiple employers in a short period of time.
    - Have a worse quality of workmanship due to reduced cognitive abilities.

- Increase criminality in the workplace to fund dependencies.
- Require micro-management by comparison with non-misusers and so on.

There is a need to avoid these on-costs to employers by preventing misusers from getting into the workplace in the first instance. A POC instant test device just does not do it. The on-cost to small employers is equally as damaging as it is to large employers. A company that screens out 100 substance misusers per year will have saved a potential on-cost to the company of £500,000 to £700,000. There is, of course, the need to then manage existing employee issues in support of the pre-employment scenario. The best way to avoid these on-costs is to have a robust and where possible planned recruiting protocol that will require more than a few hours from interview to starting work. A 5-day gap from interview to employment is a reasonable gap to cover all substance and alcohol misuse countermeasures via evidential analytical services.

16. **Knowledge of risk management.** Building a POT and an EAP allied to a legally defensible SAMP requires that a risk assessment be conducted by your supplier and your company. How can you build a bespoke SAMP, POT and EAP without that risk assessment of your company's activities and the identification of risk exposure? The fact is, a SAMP must apply to every employee regardless of position, even and especially to executive staff. In the UK it is the responsibility of the appropriate person in the company to make a fair presentation of its risk to its insurers. Since the new Insurance Act was applied in August 2016 there has been a significant increase in the denial of insurance claims within commerce and industry. Risk assessment of job- or industry-specific issues may require an escalation of what type of test medium is used and how often it is applied to those risk positions, policy development and the process of managing the risk. Remember, the policy still applies to every employee. *What are your company's risk exposures? Who knows about them? What has been done to mitigate them?*

17. **Knowledge of tendering or developing tendering processes.** It makes no difference whether you are responding to tenders or are setting tender parameters; you can apply a SAMP and POT requirement for compliance to tender. If you are tendering for a contract or a job offer, it can be conditional on a SAMP or POT being in place. Many companies apply this requirement without having a SAMP or POT in place themselves. Because of the variety of criminal and civil proceedings that can

be applied it would be a poor company that did not have the protection of a SAMP and comprehensive and robust POT to *enhance a business advantage or reputation.* A tick in the box scenario is not good enough, nor is the '*Set It and Forget It*' approach to the SAMP. There is a need in conjunction with this process to ensure that your contractors fully understand the SLA you will apply to them and the need for their own insurances to also cover this area of risk management. *What is your approach? When did you last review your SAMP, POT and EAP?*

18. **Knowledge of directors'/managers' duties and liabilities.** Many company directors, officers and managers of companies have little or no knowledge of their culpabilities or responsibilities with regard to SAMP, POT and EAP issues, including their correlation to criminality and employment law. Do you simply offer the management to another employee who tells you he or she is all fit for purpose, and have you ever challenged that approach? Sadly, too many find out when things have gone badly wrong. Culpability means the buck stops here; responsibility has a wider interpretation without necessarily leading to culpability. At Hall & Angus we believe very strongly in the well-used phrase '*Knowledge is Power*'. Training and awareness are the routes to both knowledge and power. The term power is applied so that managers will have the power to protect themselves and their staff, and directors will have the power to protect themselves, their company, their managers and their employees. Appropriate accredited training will provide the knowledge and power for employers and employees to protect themselves and their families. *Why would anyone avoid this very obvious knowledge/power benefit, regardless of position in the company?*

19. **Knowledge of Aid and Abet, Counsel or Procure offences for company directors or managers.** In the UK and within a variety of legislations, both criminal and civil, there is a provision in reference to a person to 'Aid & Abet, Counsel or Procure another in the commission of an offence.' For managers and company directors who have control over other staff activities or specific responsibilities there is a need for them to understand how a SAMP, POT and EAP can help and protect them. *What do you have in place to provide protection for this type of exposure? What is the situation in your country regarding this topic and the laws around culpable negligence?*

20. **Knowledge of the company's insurance obligations.** As of August 2016, in the UK, it is a requirement of an insurance provider to conduct a risk assessment of a company's business. It is the duty of the company to

make a fair presentation of the company's risks to its insurer. It is my opinion that workplace substance and alcohol misuse represents a risk to both parties and is required to be declared. There is a need for the insurance industry to be trained in a variety of subjects concerning workplace substance and alcohol misuse, in particular the strength and legality of the SAMP, POT and EAP and any relevant countermeasures put in place by a company. *What are the insurance requirements in your country? Are you protected as a company as well as an individual? Has your company provided you with sufficient and appropriate documented training? Have you consented to this as part of your job description or T&Cs of employment?*

21. **Knowledge of agency staff and subcontractor contracts.** When you examine the need for a workplace SAMP and POT there is a need to look at all personnel working in your facility or representing your company and its reputation on or off-site. There is no obligation for you to provide an EAP for someone else's employee. The full-time/part-time head count of company staff will all have T&Cs of employment, permanent or temporary contracts and even zero hours contracts. The fact remains, all staff have a fiduciary duty to be fit for work, and that fiduciary duty also applies to contractors. Some people take drugs, such as painkillers, to be fit for work or to have the ability to be present at work. Others take prescription medications for an existing long- or short-term illness(es), some of which have serious side effects. All of the situations in these 27 scenarios have a need to be managed regardless of what level of staff are employed – full time, agency, contractors and so on. It is for you as the company to set the standards and content of the contracts imposed on outside agencies who want to work in your environment in support of your business. It's for your agencies and subcontractors to comply with your legal directives and SLAs, especially with regard to a SAMP and POT.

22. **Knowledge of current UK or country-specific drink and drug driving regulations.** The drug driving regulations introduced into England and Wales (E&W) in 2015 state it's illegal to drive if either:

    1. You are unfit to do so because you are impaired by legal drugs or are under the influence of illegal drugs
    2. You have certain levels of illegal drugs in your blood, even if they have not affected your driving. (www.gov.uk/drug-driving-law)

    If you go back to item 19 in this list, Aid and Abet, Counsel or Procure, you will see why the England, Wales and Northern Ireland regulations have an impact on companies that have vehicles of all kinds on the roads. Why is it any different for vehicles used on site, for the use of heavy machinery, etc.? Certain questions must be asked, criteria met or test(s) need to be conducted before any staff are qualified for working in or deployed to risk areas or positions in the business. Countermeasures need to be put in place and requalification determined via medical, mental and physical wellbeing and other assessment measures. Substance and alcohol misuse testing is just one option and is recommended alongside others. There is a need for more education of staff with regard to their responsibilities and culpabilities in and away from the workplace, which can be achieved via poster campaigns; direct certificated training; enhanced induction protocols and a range of integrity/ staff handbook circulations, T&Cs of employment, etc. At Hall & Angus we believe strongly that better education about substance and alcohol misuse will lead to less testing in many situations. It also benefits employees, their families and local communities who are ultimately the employer's employment pool. *What has your company done to expand the knowledge of drink and drug driving legislations to its workforce? What are the regulations in your country?*

23. **Knowledge of how to provide and manage an Employee Assistance Programme (EAP).** You will see in the next chapter that the EAP is one of the first modules to develop within any company SAMP, POT, amnesty period or continuous employment situation. Any employee can come to an employer, at any time, to self-refer any situation that is impacting their work performance, mental and physical wellbeing and more. In the UK an employee who self-refers cannot be dismissed based on what they tell their employer about their substance or alcohol misuse and a range of other subjects. *So, what are you going to do if you do not have an EAP mechanism in place? What are your EAP enrolment and removal criteria? At what point are you going to make a decision as to that person's fitness for work/fit for purpose? What assessments have you conducted to reach any conclusion? Is the person fit for a phased return, full return, reasonable adjustment or not fit for work at all? How are you going to document this process? What is the process?* All is explained in the SAMP template documents that follow and in the specific EAP chapter.

24. **Knowledge of local communities/employment pool issues.** The demographics of drugs vary across the UK and globally. Drug profiling within your company and region is also another consideration. Substance and alcohol misusers can be anonymous in larger communities, whereas in

smaller communities everyone knows everyone else's business. Cocaine may be a big issue in one area and heroin may be an issue in another. The various strengths of cannabis are a problem everywhere. Some drugs are seasonal and become available around music festivals, the club scene and so on. Deprived low-income areas have their own issues, as do job roles that provide a high disposable income. The fact is, substance and alcohol misuse has no boundaries; it impacts all genders across all spectrums, and it does not pick and choose whom it will impact.

If any of the current governments were to proactively help the employer they would be targeting in excess of 35 million UK employees and taxpayers who are the engine room of the country's prosperity in a global market. This approach in supporting employers, in my opinion, would make local communities more buoyant and isolate 'those who want to stand outside of society's rules but be a non-compliant, non-contributing parasite within it'. The government's only answer is to tax the employee using a variety of methodologies until the day they die and leave the rest of the solutions to underfunded and understaffed public-sector solutions such as police, NHS, Criminal Justice System (CJS) and so on. It is my opinion that the government needs to consider a new approach to support the employer and the 35 million employees, as opposed to the selfish minority of individuals who do not pay taxes and do not play by the rules. This approach would surely lead to less of a strain on those public services and a rise in community cohesion with better physical and mental health support mechanisms. The workplace should become the bedrock of supporting individuals and their families.

25. **Knowledge of the workplace culture.** The workplace culture is what dictates the level of control and countermeasures applied to maintain workplace harmony and business profitability. At Hall & Angus we have developed an anonymous electronic workplace culture mapping provision which examines a range of subjects within the workplace See Chapter 6. It is designed to identify the negatives in the workplace and manage them out of the business. We then identify the workplace positives and enhance them, review all subjects year by year to measure improvement and employee and employer engagement and generate measurable new initiatives from a firm base of knowledge. A great many companies put initiatives in place that are based on perceptions, opinions or beliefs. At Hall & Angus we need to operate on the basis of fact

by elimination of those perceptions, opinions and beliefs. *What is your underlying workplace culture? How can you change it? What are you doing well? What are doing badly?*

26. **Knowledge of drugs, drug paraphernalia and a lot more.** Illegal drugs and those who misuse them have a culture and language of their own. Slang names vary from region to region in the UK as well as from country to country globally. The paraphernalia of substance misuse is openly sold in markets and shops here in the UK. At the front of this book I have compiled a small selection of commonly used drugs seized in my own area of residence, what they look like as well as paraphernalia used by misusers. Many of these pictures are courtesy of Durham Constabulary. The knowledge of drugs, paraphernalia and drug law also needs consideration with regard to signs and symptoms of drug and alcohol misuse. The only way to achieve this is via a direct training programme that can accredit the delegate across a range of subjects. While most of us have our own knowledge or experience of substance and alcohol misuse there is a growing need to understand how to manage the issue in the workplace. Many managers who are charged with handling workplace substance misuse claim to have never seen or used a drug.

27. **Knowledge of change management.** Change management is a skill in itself and very often is the first hurdle that fails. I have identified just 27 subject areas for your observation; there are many more. The provision of substance and alcohol misuse countermeasures and solutions is a very complex subject with very few experts in the field of managing a workplace situation, especially with regard to a cohesive SAMP, POT and EAP. Hopefully some of these topics covered will help you identify what change management is required, how it will be structured and applied and what the outcome will be. It is important within any change management process that there is a vehicle to quantify its progress year by year or a fast track method to identify where and why it has failed.

For the foregoing reasons and more, a POT and a policy cannot be managed from or applied if it is:

- A paragraph in a staff handbook or integrity programme.
- So verbose it cannot be defended easily in litigation.
- So brief it does not protect the company or its employees.
- Paid lip service to or a tick in the box provision.

- Put into operation without an amnesty period to allow for consultation/training/self-referral.
- Lacking commitment and communication from the company.

The company referral route to the content and management of any SAMP can vary. For larger companies, the referral route can be via the company staff handbook, integrity handbook, T&Cs of employment or employee/contractor induction protocols. This approach is not an issue as long as sufficient training and communication into the company SAMP, POT, EAP, T&Cs of employment, consents and release from liability, etc. have been provided and documented. It is essential that there is as much strategy towards testing as there is towards the policy content, and all staff must be made aware of the company's approach to and governance in such matters via a recorded and enhanced company induction protocol.

Moving forward with positive thinking

A SAMP is not a POT. It is very important to understand that a SAMP can have an extensive range of criminal, civil legislations and statutory requirements applied to it and therefore needs to be robust.

A SAMP can be defined as:

A set of identified standards that when breached have a set of consequences applied to a variety of people and situations as outlined in the SAMP.

'The next legally defensible policy we see that is not written by us will be the first.'

– Trevor Hall

A POT is not a SAMP. The POT is as bespoke to company requirements as the SAMP; Both are individual elements and just two of many that can be found within a robust and legally defensible substance and alcohol misuse package or programme.

A POT can be defined as:

'The use of a range of test mediums applied under a set of circumstances outlined to a set of people within a range of civil and criminal

legislations or as outlined in the policy and managed by the company supported by expert service providers to an agreed set of analytical standards and cut off's that have an agreed response time for result reporting.'

– Trevor Hall

The biggest problem seen within companies who do test is:

'The company using the wrong test medium, under the wrong circumstances, without a considered Service Level Agreement (SLA) in place with their service providers, all being applied and managed by untrained personnel.'

– Trevor Hall

For those companies that have no policy or POT in place there are processes to follow as outlined in the section: 'Policy development and implementation process'.

For companies that have an existing SAMP, POT and EAP

For those companies that have a SAMP, POT and EAP in place there are a variety of questions to be asked and a list of to do's that should include and help you consider a review of your existing provision:

- Update the existing policy with new legislation or as part of a routine review every 6 months or when new legislation is enacted. Your policy needs to be fluid within legislations and best practice if it is to protect you and your employees. Allocating a 2- or 3-year review date is no good when dealing with the rapid change of drugs and relevant employment and criminal laws.
- Upgrade the policy to activate new test mediums or methodologies that are not identified in the existing policy. Also consider that if you have not written a wide-window test medium into your existing policy you may want to consider applying another amnesty period particular to the window of detection before you actually start using that test medium.
- Expand the policy for compliance with statutory requirements and amendments to T&Cs of employment, especially with regard to consent.

Obtain a release from liability under a range of situations and consent of the employee that their details may be kept and processed by the laboratory or other specialist provider within the SAMP, POT and EAP.

- Find better ways to manage sector-specific requirements.
- Improve and challenge laboratory turnaround times of sample analysis.
- Comply with tender detail requested and much more.

Questions that companies should be asking on a regular basis:

- Are sample turnaround times within 48 hours or less?
- What is my current on-cost for suspending staff on full pay for longer than necessary? (Be prepared for a shock.)
- How many times has my provider failed to meet my or their SLA/Key Performance Indicators (KPIs)?
- What are my SLA and KPIs?
- When did I last meet with my provider to discuss intelligence gathered from sample results?
- When did I last meet my provider to discuss variations to my SLA or KPIs?
- When did I last challenge my provider's costs?
- Do I need to conduct further or refresher training for existing and new staff?

There are many more questions to be asked, many of which can be gathered from within the various chapters in this book.

What do you do if you DO NOT have a SAMP, POT or EAP in place?

For those companies that have nothing whatsoever in place there are a number of issues to consider first and foremost:

- Why do we need to have a SAMP in place?
- Who is the best expert service provider to appoint?
- How many providers are we going to invite to tender?

- What SLA are we going to set for sample turnaround time and toxicology reporting?
- Who will the policy apply to?
- Who will represent the company to manage the programme and liaise with the provider?
- What level of training are we prepared to apply to the company?
- Do we want expensive independent sample collection services?
- Do we want to train our own staff to conduct sample collections?
- Do we want a combination of both of the last two points?
- How do we manage a self-referral now and post-introduction of a POT?

The list can go on but make sure you are setting off on the journey for the right reasons and remember: procurement, health & safety, HR, operations, solicitors, occupational health, union representatives and others have had no formal training in how to write/build a SAMP, POT or EAP and no formal training in toxicology, laboratory processes, metabolites, cross-reactivity compounds, legal and illegal substances, investigating and much more.

Whatever you choose to do, make sure you put in place a comprehensive SLA with your service provider(s) and do not be afraid to allude to financial penalties if they do not meet your or indeed their own SLA.

Having decided to proceed with the development and implementation of a SAMP, with the subsequent POT and EAP there needs to be a **Phased Development** to follow within an agreed-on amnesty period. You cannot decide to start testing and begin immediately. If you are using all test mediums available to you, a recommended minimum amnesty period would be 90 days, which is the wide-window analytical period.

The announcement of the amnesty period should come from a senior person in the company and carry gravitas around the directive from that individual's seniority in the company.

The Hall & Angus recommended a four-phase modular approach starts with a message from a senior person in the company announcing the need to have a substance misuse programme and the company's commitment to it, such as the following.

Phase 1

(Sample announcement)

The need for a companywide Substance and Alcohol Misuse Policy and Programme of Testing

To: All.................Company Employees
From...................Senior Person in the Company
Date...................
RE: The ....Company Substance and Alcohol Misuse Policy & Programme of Testing

The company has a firm legal and moral commitment to its employees and their families to provide a safe working environment and to its customers to provide a high-quality product or level of service.

The possession, sale, use, transfer or manufacture of illegal drugs or controlled substances, and the misuse of prescribed medicines pose an unacceptable risk to the safe and efficient operations of the company and its reputation. For these reasons, the company strives to achieve and maintain a safe working environment and to continue to be an employer of choice and has the goal of a substance-free workforce. To achieve this goal we have developed an ongoing education and training programme.

In addition, employees can seek clinical intervention and professional help through the company-sponsored Employee Assistance Programme (EAP).

On ....the company will begin pre-employment and contractor testing.

On ....the company will begin using a substance and alcohol misuse testing programme relevant to all employees in line with the company Substance and Alcohol Misuse Policy (SAMP). For this to be a smooth transition and to allow those with substance or alcohol dependency issues to come forward and confidentially self-refer an issue, a 90-day amnesty period will commence for all existing employees.

The 90 day amnesty period begins....................................

The company and its officers have a legal duty to comply with a variety of civil and criminal legislations with regard to substance and alcohol misuse issues and we strongly encourage employees to seek assistance from the EAP for any substance misuse or alcohol problem before reaching a point where their judgement, performance, behaviour or positive drug test has led to disciplinary action.

Signed

> *Note: This company memo from a senior person will be generated as a result of the tendering process being completed and the appointment of the provider who will work in partnership with the company to provide total management support to all aspects of workplace substance and alcohol misuse countermeasures. Indeed, the content of this memo should be derived from discussions with your chosen provider.*

Phase 2

Phase 2 has a number of elements that may have already been put into motion before the Phase 1 announcement. Phase 1, as stated, usually follows on from the appointment of an appropriate provider who will already be guiding the company, hopefully through the Hall & Angus four-phase approach to testing and implementation of a company SAMP, POT and EAP.

Within the early days of Phase 2 the following 12 steps are the minimum that should be taken. More can be added at the request of the company or service provider, and these can be company or sector-specific. The following items are for your minimum consideration:

1. The identification and make-up of an implementation committee/persons, which should include union and works council representatives alongside other designated personnel
2. The name of the service provider supporting the company programme
3. The start date of an agreed amnesty period for consultation and self-referral of those existing staff with thus-far undeclared dependencies/issues
4. The start date for the testing of existing staff

Note: New start employees have no contract and therefore they can be tested from the beginning of their pre-employment process and have updated T&Cs of employment applied. This rule can also apply to contractors.

5. The building of an Employee Assistance Programme (EAP). This is a critical first step as it will require, post-announcement, that the company is in a position to legally manage those staff who subsequently self-refer. See Chapter 4.
6. A template document/pamphlet for communicating the details of the company policy to shift briefings, Q&A sessions, notice boards, internal intranet, etc.
7. A template policy for further development and to be bespoke to your company by the service provider working with the implementation committee/team.
8. A template SAMP, POT and EAP management manual to contain general information as well as Standard Operating Procedures (SOPs) for sample collection across all selected test mediums.
9. Training of the implementation committee/team in test mediums; awareness of managing and implementing a SAMP, POT, and EAP; signs and symptoms of workplace and employee substance and alcohol misuse; chain of custody and so on.
10. The creation of briefing sessions to all staff and all shift patterns for Q&A's as applied via the company communication document. Do not be afraid to have your provider present at shift briefings; it is as important for them as it is for you to gauge the employee response and concerns, if any.
11. Regular service provider/committee meetings, as there is a need to agree and understand which test mediums are to be used by the company. Be guided by the service provider's advice but be aware:
    - Not all laboratories use the same equipment or processes.
    - Not all hair testing is the same.
    - There are some serious considerations around the management of a non-observed urine sample collection.
    - If you decide on urine as your narrow-window primary test medium you will still need a saliva provision for those situations in which a donor cannot pass urine within a specified time or is deliberately withholding the specimen.

- If you decide on saliva as your narrow-window primary test medium, you will still need urine for those donors who suffer from dry mouth syndrome or other associated medical conditions.
- Some laboratories will analyze only the kits they sell.
- Some providers do not believe in or can provide the total management you may be looking for.
- Research what test mediums can and cannot do and be sure you are setting achievable goals. See Chapter 2.

12. Agree on the SLA with your selected service provider and the contracted analytical laboratories to ensure turnaround times of samples are not exceeded and toxicology reports are both clear and concise. Set what KPIs you want to develop to help you monitor your POT and EAP. Hall & Angus has an electronic result map that will break down tests by site, shift, department, drug and more. Remember that it's the toxicology report that will help you make the decision about an individual's future with the company. Be in no doubt of what the report is saying.

Template policy information booklet/information document

This part of Phase 2 can be developed as a booklet for all staff to have and sign for. It can be promulgated at notice boards and canteens, discussed at shift briefings or it can simply be added to the Phase 4 operation; the choice is yours. It is important to remember that this information, after the initial announcement, is usually one of the first comprehensive indications or communications of the company's approach to managing its employees within the company SAMP, POT and EAP.

Hall & Angus template pamphlet

About the Company Substance and Alcohol Misuse Policy

Programme of Testing and Employee Assistance Programme

Introduction

The inappropriate use of substances like alcohol, illegal drugs, legally prescribed drugs, psychoactive substances and other substances can have a damaging effect not only on the individual concerned but also on those they make contact with at work, socially and at home.

The company has no desire to interfere with your private life. You should, however, understand that the psychological and physical effects of alcohol, drugs and other substances which affect behaviour, impair judgement/cognitive abilities and exhibit mental health and general wellbeing issues could inadvertently be brought to the workplace. There is a *Fiduciary Duty* on the part of any employee to be *Fit for Work* while engaged in their company duties and in compliance with their terms and conditions of employment.

As a responsible employer we have a moral and legal duty to provide as safe an environment as is reasonably practicable for all of our employees and to ensure the safety of our customers, contractors, visitors and the public. This requires that the company and its officers comply with a variety of criminal and civil legislations that are constantly applied and monitored for change.

To maintain an adequate insurance cover for our business we are obliged to make a fair presentation of company risks to our insurers, we consider the misuse of substances and alcohol as a risk which has to be managed within our company operations and disclosed to our insurers.

For these reasons the company is introducing measures that are in effective for *all* employees which will actively encourage staff to manage their lives in such a way that everyone's safety at work is not jeopardized. The same standards are also applicable to our contractors and visitors.

This information forms part of a committed programme of awareness that will be provided to all employees and will include:

1. A formal policy which clearly states the company's standards and procedures regarding alcohol and substance misuse.
2. An outline of the consequences of breaching the policy.
3. Information which allows employees to make responsible decisions regarding the use of alcohol and other substances.
4. A formal POT.
5. Advice and guidance to employees who require assistance in dealing with an alcohol/substance misuse problem or other treatable dependencies.
6. Where to obtain further information.

Note: The introduction may vary from sector to sector and company to company. Be clear about what you are telling your staff, contractors and visitors. Be clear what you will apply to tenders, procurement specifications and much more.

The need for a policy

1. The company wishes to promote the safety of our staff, contractors and customers.
2. The risks to health & safety concerning the misuse of alcohol, illegal and prescribed drugs and psychoactive substances cannot be ignored.
3. To comply with a variety of criminal and civil legislations.
4. The company to protect its reputation while becoming an employer of choice and provide a safe working environment.

Note: As with the introduction be clear about your needs for a policy.

About the company policy

1. Applies to everyone.
2. Provides firm guidelines, which are in line with current industry best practice.
3. Provides a confidential route to and a provision for intervention programmes for anyone who thinks they require help with a drug or alcohol problem/addiction of any kind.
4. Outlines test mediums and alcohol limits to be employed by the company.

Note: Remember the proposed definition of a policy and keep the need to that level. General information (GI) has no part to play in the policy. GI is kept out of this document and is made available in the SAMP, POT and EAP Administration Manual.

About the Programme of Testing (POT)

The limits – alcohol

The breath alcohol legal limit in England and Wales for drivers is:

Breath alcohol = **35** micrograms per 100 millilitres of breath is the official measure in the UK.

In Scotland the limit is **22** micrograms per 100 millilitres of breath.

The company workplace limit is.............

> *Note: Setting the company limit below the legal drink drive limit is your choice, except where mandated by law. Remember, in the case of alcohol you are dealing with a legal substance and your disciplinary approach can be a more considered approach to disciplinary action that does not need to go directly to summary dismissal.*

The limits – drugs

Any use, possession or trafficking of illegal drugs or anabolic steroids and the misuse, whether intentional or not, of prescription drugs, over-the-counter (OTC) medicine, psychoactive substances, glues, gasses, aerosols and solvents is prohibited. All relevant civil and criminal legislations apply to the company substance misuse policy.

Anyone taking prescribed or OTC medication must always follow the dosage instructions carefully. Employees must inform the company HR or health & safety department (this will be confidential) of those or other substances that cause severe drowsiness or impair reflexes or cognitive abilities to ensure their safety and that of others is not compromised.

It is incumbent upon any GP or pharmacist to inform users of any side effects of prescribed medication that may impair your abilities and judgement. It is equally incumbent for an employee to declare any side effects of any substances that impede their ability to perform their duties or that could expose the company to prosecution under a variety of circumstances.

Note: Set your limits and standards within a set of guidelines laid down by industry or your own requirements if you wish them to be more or less restrictive.

Enforcement of the policy

The company must exercise due diligence as well as protect itself and its directors and managers from criminal and civil litigations in the execution of their duties and the laws of the land in which the company operates. A key part of the substance and alcohol misuse policy is the enforcement of the limits set within a variety of civil and criminal legislations as well as any limits set by the company policy.

Competent persons can be trained in-house to administer the alcohol breath testing/drug testing processes using approved testing devices and methods agreed to by the company.

An external professional agency can also be contacted for the independent collection of breath alcohol testing and or hair/fingernail clippings/urine/oral fluid drug testing. Their representatives are fully trained and certified to carry out such tests using approved testing products and procedures, which provide accurate toxicology reporting.

Note: When looking at the enforcement of the policy there is a need to examine the level of training provided to those who are an integral part of the disciplinary decision-making process.

Testing

The company may choose to conduct testing in the following situations:

1. Pre-employment
2. For cause/post incident
3. Internal investigation
4. Under the influence

5. Follow up: random or rotational testing
6. Pre-promotion
7. Rehabilitation testing
8. Return to work testing
9. Relocation or secondment to another company
10. Job/contractor specific

Testing can be considered in other situations not listed above. Items 1–10 are for considered guidance.

You may face dismissal if you:

1. Consume illegal drugs or misuse legal substances, psychoactive substances or alcohol while on duty or at a client's premises or on company business.
2. You are in possession or found to be trafficking illegal drugs, psychoactive substances, prescribed medications, anabolic steroids or black market substances while on company duty.
3. Screen positive for illegal drugs, psychoactive substances or misuse of prescribed medications following laboratory analysis.
4. Refuse or obstruct the provision of an alcohol breath sample or substance misuse test on a company-approved device.
5. Decline to take or miss an approved course of treatment (appointment) related to a drug and/or alcohol problem if advised to do so by the company.
6. Misuse legally prescribed medications or are in illegal possession of prescribed medications.

Note: Where prescription drugs are found to be present in any screen or confirmation analysis, the donor will be required to provide the prescription as evidence of medicines legally prescribed by a GP.

Note: The whole theme of this document is the 'you may' approach when highlighting consequences. The policy document is more of a 'you will' type of document.

Frequently asked questions and answers

Q. Where can I read a copy of the policy?

A. A copy of the policy is available from the company upon request and at the point of testing.

Q. I know I have a problem, but do not want to lose my job. What should I do?

A. It is in everybody's interest, especially yours, to come forward to get help before the policy is implemented. There are many independent agencies that can help. If you don't come forward for help and you then test positive for drugs and/or alcohol, this can be dealt with under the company disciplinary procedure or by way of a reasonable adjustment under the Equality Act 2010 and entry into the company Employee Assistance Programme (EAP).

Q. I do drink alcohol, so how many can I have?

A. It depends on the individual, gender, size, weight, frequency, etc. The guidelines are that one unit of alcohol takes 1 hour to clear from your system.

Q. What is one unit of alcohol?

A. A half-pint of ordinary strength beer, lager or cider, a single pub measure of spirits or a single medium glass of wine.

Q. Is testing an infringement of my civil rights?

A. In the pursuit of a safe workplace, drug and alcohol misuse is a legally recognized hazard. As such it is legally incumbent on the company to reduce the risk by having a properly framed Company Substance and Alcohol Misuse Policy, which will include testing by the best methods currently available. This may cause inconvenience to the person being tested, but as testing is carried out for legitimate objectives, bearing in mind the nature of the company's business, and with respect for the rights of individual employees, it will not breach your rights under the Human Rights Act 1998.

Q. How long do drugs stay in my system?

A. Drugs stay in the system for varying times dependent on the type of drug, purity of the drug and how often the drug is misused. The recovery of drugs from a donor will vary with the type of collection medium used, for example:

1. Drug metabolite stays in head and body hair permanently and pro-portionate to use Each half inch of head hair equates to an approxi-mately 30-day history. Body hair grows at a slower rate and therefore has a wider window of detection.
2. In saliva most drug metabolites can be discovered within 6 hours of ingestion and are recoverable for 24 hours or more depending on the purity of drug and regularity of use.
3. In urine drug metabolites are recoverable for a 1–5-day window, with cannabis possibly being recoverable up to 28 days, again depending on the purity of drug used and the regularity of use.
4. Variations occur based on the regularity of use and the purity or type of drug.
5. Depending on the type and purity of the drug used there are a vari-ety of durations for which the individual drug is active and the donor is under the influence or impaired.
6. Impairment has a variety of reactions and durations depending on whether the abuser is using multiple drugs at the same time or mixing illegal drugs with prescribed/OTC medication or with alcohol/other substances.

Q. I take prescribed medication and buy OTC medication. Will I test positive under the company drug testing programme?

A. If your sample is collected using urine or saliva it can test positive for opi-ates and other substances. If in these circumstances your sample screens positive your employer is obliged to send the result for further analysis to an accredited laboratory. Mass spectrometry will identify the exact drug metabolite and a cut-off level in line with industry and medicinal guidelines. You can be assured the cut-off levels for prescription or OTC medicines are well below those for illegal substances. There are also other compounds that are found in illegal substances that are not found in legally prepared prescription or OTC medicines.

Q. What are legal highs? And do they form part of the company SAMP?

A. Legal highs were sold in the UK and labelled 'NOT FIT FOR HUMAN CONSUMPTION' or 'PLANT FOOD'. These substances are now illegal and are covered under the Psychoactive Substances Act 2016. As such they do form part of the company substance misuse programme and are applied also to the company disciplinary procedures.

> Note: This pamphlet/phase, as stated, can be produced for issue to full-time and part-time employees. If so make sure it is signed for and a document about its issue is placed into the person's HR file. It should always be presented as part of an enhanced induction process around multiple topics. If it remains part of the induction process or T&Cs of employment there are forms to sign that are in the back of the Administration section of this chapter that are relevant to the UK's GDPR (General Data Protection Guidelines).

A Phase 2 tick sheet

Use this checklist and add anything else you think appropriate before you move to Phase 3.

1. Has the announcement been made to all staff from a senior person with regard to the start date of the amnesty period?
2. Has the start date of the substance and alcohol misuse programme been circulated to all staff?
3. Have all contractors and recruitment protocols been informed of the start date of the company testing programme relevant to their activities/appointment? Remember, new employees, contractors and visitors can be tested immediately.
4. Is the Employee Assistance Programme in place and activated?
5. Has the implementation committee been trained?
6. Has the 'About the Company Substance and Alcohol Misuse Policy and Programme of Testing' document been circulated or promulgated?
7. Have shift briefings been conducted?
8. Have the test mediums and the date they will be applied been selected?
9. Has the company Substance and Alcohol Misuse Policy and Programme of Testing been finalized?
10. Have Phases 3 and 4 of the Policy and Policy Management Document been started?

Post issue and completion of the above tasks

Once Phase 2 has been completed, usually within the first month of announcement, the development of Phase 3 will have already commenced in part, usually as a result of regular service provider/committee meetings.

Phase 3

Phase 3 is the build/finalization of the policy itself and will cover any additional sector- or company-specific variances from this template. This is the most important document and the only one that will or may be challenged in litigation. At this stage it may be worth the larger companies having a direct input from legal counsel or the compliance department. In any event a legal expert should have a view of the policy document once finished, not least of all to ensure there are no unnecessary risk exposures to the company or its employees. In all situations, the final policy should be signed off by a legal representative of the company so that it aligns with corporate/company governance and vice versa.

Template Company

Substance and Alcohol Misuse Policy (SAMP)

1. Purpose

This policy outlines to every employee, contractor and visitor the company's considered approach to substance/drug/alcohol misuse. It also makes clear the company's approach to interventions.

> *Note: It is a simple statement of what is a complicated topic; the above is both concise and accurate. Remember, interventions can be clinical as well as disciplinary.*

2. Policy

It is the company's policy to:

(a) Ensure that the use of illegal drugs/substances, legally prescribed medications, psychoactive substances, anabolic steroids or alcohol by employees, contractors or visitors does not affect the health & safety of the individuals themselves, their fellow workers or others with whom they come into contact in the course of their work.

(b) Ensure that an employee's, contractor's or visitor's use of illegal drugs or legally prescribed medications or illegal use of prescribed medication, psychoactive substances, alcohol or other substances and vapours does not affect the efficient and effective operation of the company's business and that employees, contractors and visitors are fit for their respective positions/contracts on or away from company premises while on duty or visiting with the company.

(c) Provide a confidential procedure whereby employees who have a problem of substance or alcohol misuse or other dependency issues can seek help in confidence within the workplace or in private.

(d) Establish a process for handling such issues through the company-sponsored Employee Assistance Programme (EAP).

(e) Provide guidance on the effects of illegal drugs, psychoactive substances, prescribed medications, alcohol and other dependencies that may impair their judgement and fitness for work.

> *Note: Be clear about what your policy is and what it is you want to make clear to employees, contractors and visitors to your business. Remember, general information is not policy.*

3. Principles

(a) It is the company's responsibility to implement this policy in line with expert support and a considered approach to such matters. Implementation will involve full communication and consultation with employees via a company-appointed implementation team. Relevant amnesty periods for existing employees will be enforced and full certificated training will be provided for designated staff.

(b) The company encourages any employee with a substance, alcohol or other dependency problem to inform the company in confidence, particularly if it is being reflected in poor work performance, poor judgement and other issues that may impact the company or the employee.

(c) No person with an alcohol, substance or other dependency problem will have his or her job security or promotional opportunity jeopardized by a request for an agreed intervention, diagnosis, treatment or enrolment into an agreed rehabilitation or Employee Assistance Programme (EAP).

(d) Individuals who do not seek or comply with a treatment regime will *not* be considered favourably should they raise a dependency problem as mitigating circumstances during any disciplinary action, at the time a test is requested of them or during an internal investigation. The confidential nature of the medical records of individuals with an alcohol or substance dependency will be preserved under the Data Protection Act and by record control of outside agencies employed by this company.

(e) Individuals participating in a rehabilitation programme or EAP will, in the first instance, be expected to meet existing or agreed job performance standards and established work rules and policies. In the event the treatment or the condition referred requires a reasonable adjustment to a new role the employee will be removed to that role and the appropriate pay grade of the role. The company takes a serious view of the misuse of alcohol and other substances which impact the performance of the individual or the reputation of the company. Where individuals fall foul of the disciplinary procedure in line with this policy, most serious action will be taken, up to and including dismissal.

(f) Nothing in this statement of policy is to be interpreted as constituting a waiver of the company and its Designated Employee Representative (DER) responsibility to maintain discipline, or the right to take disciplinary measures in the case of poor performance or misconduct that may result from alcohol/substance dependency or misuse issues, whether illegal or prescribed drugs.

> *Note: The principles of the policy need to reflect a range of the other governances of the company, especially how the company will or will not assist its employees and subsequently deliver the process into the workplace.*

4. Definitions

Alcohol and substance misuse issues can be defined by the following categories:

1. Alcohol dependence/excessive alcohol consumption/intoxication.
2. Being under the influence, taking, trafficking or possessing illegal drugs or psychoactive substances on company premises or during company time.
3. Misuse and/or distribution of legal substances such as prescribed medicines and anabolic steroids. Includes the need to notify the company of any impairment from the use of prescribed drugs, especially where drink and drug driving regulations may be enforced against the company or any of its employees while on company business.
4. Substance dependency is a condition in which an employee's consumption of any substance(s) occurs frequently or repeatedly and interferes with his or her health, attitude to safety, attendance or general work performance.
5. Substance intoxication is defined by the company as excessive consumption which may result in irresponsible behaviour/judgement but which is not necessarily related to a physical or psychological dependence.

Mental health, physical wellbeing or psychological dependence must be identified or eliminated in an EAP, and as such any individual enrolled in such a programme will be required to submit to either or both examinations by the company's appointed and qualified representative. The goals of the EAP will be to establish a recovery-oriented treatment programme to identify a treatment history and any unmet needs and then develop a treatment profile and a treatment outcome.

Note: Definitions help you identify what the company will not tolerate and the measure by which you achieve those decisions.

5. Standards of behaviour and performance while on duty on and off company premises

5.1 Consumption of alcohol during company time

(a) Employees and contractors must not consume alcohol on the company's premises except at authorized official functions. Any breach of this rule by employees or contractors will result in a hearing under the company's disciplinary procedure which could lead to dismissal or the contractor's removal from site or contract.

(b) Where company employees or its representatives are visiting with potential or existing customers those employees or representatives must act in such a way as to not bring the company's reputation into question or breach any of the company's policies contained in this document as well as the other company policies.

(c) Failure to observe these rules will result in a hearing under the company's disciplinary procedure which could lead to summary dismissal or a contractor's removal from site or contract.

> *Note: Standards of behaviour are the DNA of your company's reputation with regard to substance and alcohol misuse.*

5.2 Drug/alcohol/substance misuse or possession on the premises

(a) Employees and contractors must not use, be under the influence of or in the possession of illegal drugs, alcohol or substances which have not been prescribed on medical grounds while on company premises/business. Failure to observe this rule will result in a hearing under the company's disciplinary procedure which could lead to summary dismissal or the contractor's removal from site or contract.

(b) The company reserves the right to conduct investigations into on-site substance, drug and alcohol misuse, whether illegal, prescribed, black market or over the counter, and of use of other substances that are psychoactive or that impair judgement and physical demeanour. This may include personal, locker and vehicle searches and any other steps to prevent criminality/harm/abuse in the workplace.

(c) With regard to the use of prescribed medicines, illicit drugs or other substances off-site, the company will remind employees, contractors and visitors alike of the need to comply with drug driving regulations in England and Wales. Any employee or contractor who has been convicted of any offence under UK drug/drink driving regulations must inform the company where the conviction has resulted in the loss of a driving licence or submission into any treatment programme or high-risk offender's scheme.

Note: This section sets the standards by which you are compelled by civil and criminal legislations to take certain courses of actions. Employees, contractors, visitors and the tenders you set should cover these and possibly other sector-specific laws/standards

5.3 Employee/contractor performance

Employees or contractors who take substances that affect their work performance or judgement, or demonstrate other recordable behaviours such as impaired or unusual demeanour, will be subject to the company's substance misuse testing programme and disciplinary procedure up to and including dismissal or removal from site or contract.

Note: This section should be part of the contractors' T&Cs and made very clear to them on appointment. For visitors, there should be some form of notification to read, as is done with regard to fire evacuation or accident reporting.

5.4 Standards

(a) It should be noted that the testing methods used by the company can identify the use of substances in the past 90 days or more and that employees are expected to be free from all illegal substances at the time of any test being administered. Due consideration will be given to each positive test as it comes to the notice of the company and its management team.

(b) The company reserves the right to use a range of drug and alcohol testing mediums supported by a variety of interventions and application of a variety of civil and criminal legislations.

(c) The company is obliged to declare substance and alcohol misuse as part of its risk assessment and declaration to its insurer so that appropriate insurance coverage is provided in the protection of the company's business activities by its employees, visitors, contractors and exposure to criminal and civil legislations.

(d) The company will use only a relevant accredited laboratory for its analytical services. All test kits used will be regulated under a variety of Medicines and Healthcare products Regulatory Agency (MHRA) and other clinical regulations appropriate to that type of test kit.

(e) With regard to workplace test limits (cut-offs), the company will adhere to the European Workplace Drug Testing Society (EWDTS) cut-offs for normal testing protocols. Lower levels (healthcare cut-offs) may be used during enrolment into a company-sponsored EAP.

(f) Scotland has its own cut-off for breath-testing devices when compared with the rest of the UK. The company reserves the right to set its own limit in line within its corporate governance. The company's cut-off is.....................

Note: This section alerts all staff, contractors and visitors to the company's approach for the Programme Of Testing (POT).

6. Process

6.1 Establishing the problem

Supervisors and managers should be aware that the misuse of drugs and alcohol by employees may come to light in various ways. The following are some of the indicators, especially when identified in combinations that may suggest the presence of an alcohol- or substance-related problem.

Absenteeism	Poor productivity
Employee criminality	Poor product quality
Accidents	Poor customer service
Compensation claims	Discipline
Workplace violence	Rehabilitation costs

Please note these are just some of the indicators and should not be used in isolation.

> **Note: This section indicates some of the considerations that may instigate the POT and it is for the company to extend or apply these issues when enforcing the SAMP.**

6.2 Some company testing applications

(a) Pre-employment
(b) For cause/Post-incident
(c) Random or rotational, with or without notice
(d) Job-specific, promotion or relocation
(e) Follow-up
(f) Self-referral
(g) Return to work
(h) Under the influence at work/reasonable suspicion/third-party referral
(i) Substantiated anonymous information
(j) Demeanour and reasonable suspicion
(k) Contract-/job-specific

> **Note: This section identifies the majority of situations in which testing can be applied within the SAMP.**

6.3 Testing

Various methods of testing will be available and carried out by authorized and suitably qualified personnel.

Note: This section, as brief as it is, outlines the very important fact that the company reserves the right to use a variety of methodologies for testing. This section is also available for expansion to allow for sector-specific content such as railway, air and marine transport laws/processes.

7. Treatment

The following are some optional elements in arranging treatment:

(a) Normal sick pay or statutory sick pay provisions will apply for absence arising due to treatment.
(b) A fixed payment term and time scale will be set for such treatment.
(c) The individual will provide random samples following their return to work for an agreed period of time.
(d) The employee(s) will normally be able to return to the same or equivalent work.
(e) The employer may make reasonable adjustments to facilitate your treatment programme within the company's EAP.

Note: This section is necessary to cover the company's approach to managing those employees who develop a need for a treatment programme and the manner by which the programme will be managed.

7.1 Relapses

Where an employee, having received treatment, suffers a relapse, the matter will be handled under the company's disciplinary procedure; however, the company will consider each case on individual merits. Medical advice will be sought in an attempt to ascertain how much more treatment/rehabilitation time is likely to be required for a full or structured recovery. In very rare cases and at the company's discretion, more treatment or rehabilitation time may be given in order to help the employee to recover fitness for work.

Note: This section and 7.2 highlight the consequences of relapse and recovery unlikely scenarios. Section 7.1 may have more latitude towards a second chance or extension of an existing treatment programme or the employee going back into a restructured second programme of treatment.

7.2 Recovery unlikely

If, after an employee has received treatment, recovery seems unlikely, the company may decide to end the individual's employment.

8. Drug and alcohol searches on company property

The company has zero tolerance of criminality in the workplace and therefore requires that employee lockers, vehicles, bags and outer clothing may be searched for evidence of illegal drugs and other criminal activity suspected on company property. Searches can be random or part of an internal investigation.

Refusal to submit to a company search for illegal drugs, alcohol and other criminal activity can lead to disciplinary action up to and including dismissal.

Any employee, contractor or visitor discovered with or found to be using illegal drugs on company property will be reported to the police immediately. Visitor and contractor searches will be conducted under the same guidelines.

Note: This section is very important and sets out one or more of the overt countermeasures being applied by the company on company premises.

Phase 4

Phase 4 of the programme is the development of the administration manual for the management of the SAMP, POT and EAP. This document should contain

1. **General information** about substance and alcohol misuse that is not policy

2. **The Standard Operating Procedures (SOPs)** for managing the donor and the collection protocols and countermeasures for

- Collecting a breath sample
- Collecting a hair or fingernail clippings sample
- Collecting a saliva sample
- Collecting a urine sample
- Maintaining chain of custody across all collections, to include recording of consent
- Incident reporting documents designed specifically for the company
- EAP consent and compliance documents
- Documents generic to the company
- Any other document or processes that are not policy but the company wants to develop for the management of the whole programme

The policy guidance manual can be made available to any employee to view but not at the time of a request for an employee to submit to a drug or alcohol test. It is only the policy that should be offered to the potential donor. The same is true of the pamphlet which is titled 'About the Company Substance and Alcohol Misuse Policy and Programme of Testing'. All too often companies combine all phases and have a policy that is 40–60 pages long; bear this in mind when you have to allow employees the right to read the policy and require they sign to say they have read and understood the policy. The induction process should allow for each of these phased documents to be reviewed and where necessary trained and signed for.

Template

Substance and Alcohol Misuse Policy

Programme of Testing and Employee Assistance Programme

Administration Manual

1. Types of testing

The company requires testing under a number of circumstances, which can include:

Pre-employment testing

All prospective employees can be required to undertake and pass pre-employment testing.

The company has identified the need for a drug- and alcohol-free workplace and has identified pre-employment testing as a means to prevent the migration of substance misuse into the workplace, which has a quantifiable negative cost impact of employing individuals who are involved in such misuse and are not undergoing a form of treatment.

For-cause testing

Post-accident/incident testing is carried out when an accident/incident occurs and there are reasonable grounds to suspect that the actions or omissions of an employee led to the accident. This process may be undertaken as part of the accident investigation procedures or as a need to comply with the company's insurance risk assessment and risks the company has declared within that policy.

For-cause testing can also arise when there is reasonable suspicion that an employee has been misusing alcohol or substances. All incidents in which an employee(s) is or is suspected to be breaching criminal or recognized civil legislation will also be treated as a for-cause incident. If an employee displays behaviour, appearance or odour that leads a member of management to reasonably believe that the employee may be acting under the influence of intoxicating liquor or substance misuse, the employee will be taken to a suitable location where the appropriate procedure will be initiated.

Random or rotational testing

The company recognizes that if the need arises, the company may conduct a policy of random testing. This could involve the random screening of company employees throughout the year. Full consultation would take place with employees to communicate the process, the random manner of selection and the method of handling the results, all of which would fall within the scope of this procedure.

Job-specific, promotion or relocation testing

This will occur when an employee is being promoted or relocated to another job position or another facility or company location. The company also reserves the right to drug test staff who have been selected for a specific job which requires a high-risk assessment, promotion or relocation to another facility or location within the parent company/subsidiary or on secondment to another company.

Follow-up testing

An employee who has been tested positive for drugs or alcohol may be subject to further periodic testing to ensure that the employee is complying with any course of rehabilitation that has been prescribed (e.g. where a candidate has completed or is still in a rehabilitation programme and it is necessary to check progress).

Self-referral

1. If anyone approaches the company for assistance, the individual will be referred to a medical practitioner or equivalent, or a rehabilitation programme; or an Employee Assistance Programme (EAP) will be set up. This will be done in confidence. The employee will be examined and an appropriate intervention programme identified and initiated by agreement.
2. Where there is a clear risk to health & safety, management may reallocate the employee to other duties in an approach of reasonable accommodation. If this is not possible the individual will be treated as sick and the company or statutory sick pay policy will apply.
3. If the individual fails subsequently to adhere to any rehabilitation or EAP programme, or fails to meet work standards, or relapses into a situation in which rehabilitation is unlikely or becomes protracted beyond an agreed-on intervention time period this will be dealt with in the disciplinary procedure up to and including dismissal.
4. The consent declaration document is required to be completed by the employee and a company representative authorized to consider and start such a programme of an employee wishing to self-refer. In particular, the inclusion and exclusion criteria need to be considered prior to the signing of the body of the consent page.

Hall & Angus sample consent document

Enrolment into the company EAP (SOP no.)

I.. employee no .... wish to self-refer into the company Employee Assistance Programme (EAP). I declare that the issues I have confidentially outlined to the HR department are having an impact on my mental/physical/general wellbeing. I am aware of the inclusion and exclusion criteria (overleaf), the implications of which have been explained to me. I am also aware that the EAP may also include the employer's rights to impose the government's Fit for Work programme. I am prepared to submit to a recovery-oriented treatment programme supported by clinical interventions where necessary that are appointed from within the company programme. I will further notify my GP of my enrolment into the EAP and ask that they support the programme provider and my employer with any requested medical records or information.

I will support the company and its treatment providers in the provision of my past and current treatment history and respond to any identified unmet need that may require additional support.

I am aware that my current role may need to be changed to facilitate a reasonable adjustment while I am enrolled in the company EAP.

I am prepared to submit to regular treatment effectiveness reviews while on the EAP and am aware that any unqualified obstruction or refusal to meet their needs can result in removal from the EAP to the detriment of my position within the company up to and including dismissal.

Signed...Date............................

Print name...Position................................

Witnessed...Date............................

Print name...Position................................

Before signing see over/below for exclusion and removal criteria

Exclusion criteria:

The manner of referral may not be appropriate under the circumstances of the need to refer, e.g.

- *Circumstances that lead to the self-referral were preceded by a criminal act or act of gross misconduct within the company (company decision).*
- *Where substance misuse was discovered prior to self-referral, post-test, etc.*
- *Where the company disciplinary process has already been activated.*
- *Where the problem referred was already a statutory requirement under the Road Traffic Act (Driver and Vehicle Licensing Agency) or part of an existing treatment programme which has statutory requirements attached to it.*
- *Employee refuses to enrol in the programme when an issue has been identified.*

Removal criteria

The removal criteria may be activated when a person who is enrolled in the company EAP:

- *Obstructs, in whole or in part of the EAP treatment/intervention requirements.*
- *Fails to attend without reasonable cause any treatment sessions or specialist interventions.*
- *After due consideration it is decided that recovery is unlikely.*
- *Relapses to a previous reason to enrol into the programme.*
- *Leaves the company.*
- *Fails without reasonable cause to adhere to a GP or programme provider's advice and guidance.*

Note: The company reserves the right to add to or remove any of the above criteria as and when the need arises or the nature of civil or criminal legislations changes.

Monitoring of employees post-EAP

Depending on the report(s) of the treatment provider and in agreement with the employee certain situations will require monitoring for an agreed period of time, which may be up to 2 years in duration.

Continued monitoring is required for some dependencies and forms part of a complete treatment programme designed for the benefit of the employee and the company; e.g. where a drug misuser/dependent has or continues to be rehabilitated there is a need for the benefit of the employee and the company to continue random testing protocols to ensure the employee does not relapse or is in a continued recovery programme.

The company reserves the right to employ a variety of methods to monitor employees who are enrolled in the company EAP. Where paid absence is available the company will remind those who are enrolled in the EAP that they continue to be employees of the company while absent from the workplace. Accordingly, paid absence requires that terms and conditions of the employee's contract of employment are enforceable.

Any activities of the employee that delay the return or extend the need for treatment will invoke the company disciplinary procedure. Any cost volunteered by the company to the employee's treatment programme will be stopped and may be recovered from salary.

Return to work

The company reserves the right to test staff who are returning to work after a protracted period of absenteeism. Each case will be judged separately.

Under the influence at work/reasonable suspicion

1. This section is specifically for dealing with any individual on-site who is believed to be under the influence of intoxicating liquor or substance misuse, or appears to be so.
2. If any employee, visitor or contractor displays behaviour, appearance or odour that leads a member of management to believe reasonably that the employee may be acting under the influence of intoxicating liquor or

substance misuse, the employee will be taken to a suitable location and the relevant testing protocol will then take place.

3. In the event the employee or contractor refuses to participate, they should be sent home pending a disciplinary hearing or contractor meeting. The failure to participate in the testing will be taken into account at that hearing.

(Management must ensure suitable safe means of getting the employee/visitor/ contractor home and bear in mind the need to comply with UK drink and drug driving legislation.)

Third-party referral/management investigation

1. Employees may be tested for drugs or intoxicating liquor after any accident, incident or occurrence where there are reasonable grounds to suspect that it was due to the acts or omissions of the employee(s).
2. The company may introduce a policy of random or rotational testing where a problem of dependency or misuse is thought to exist.
3. Where a person is reasonably thought to have, or appear to have, a dependency or addiction problem, management will follow the appropriate testing/intervention procedures.
4. Offer assistance for the dependency or addiction by seeing a medical practitioner, specialist case worker or equivalent, to set up a rehabilitation programme within an agreed EAP.
5. Failure to meet any of the above will make the employee liable to more serious disciplinary action up to and including dismissal.

Prescribed/non-prescription medicines

Employees, and where required contractors, must provide information to their line manager or the Human Resources manager regarding their current use of prescribed/non-prescription medicines that may affect their capacity to safely and effectively undertake the duties of their post and to meet the legal requirements for driving on a UK road (where appropriate). This information will be dealt with in the strictest confidence. It will enable your GP to prescribe an alternative medicine that will not have side effects that impact your job description, your safety and the safety of your work colleagues while at work. Details required may consist of:

- Post held by employee
- Contract necessity
- Details of prescription/medicine
- Dosage
- Medical condition
- Details of prescribing medical practitioner
- Precautionary advice printed on the label

It is important to note that where an individual is prescribed medicine by a doctor or pharmacist, the company reserves the right to ensure that the medicines being taken will not negatively impact safe working. Where it is considered to do so, the person may, for the safety of others and themselves, be assigned alternative work, or suspended from work on medical grounds. Payment during such suspension will be in line with local sick pay agreements. Return to work will be considered only upon receipt of a written clearance from a medical practitioner and a review of the risk by the company.

1. Alcohol testing

Introduction

There are different methods of testing for intoxicating liquor in the body. Testing generally relies on breath testing. To dispel any doubts over the validity of the testing methods, the company uses methods of testing that are employed in the UK and elsewhere in Europe using equipment approved by the company. The UK legal limit for drivers is

Blood: 80 mg (milligrams) of alcohol per 100-ml (millilitres) of blood
Breath: 35 mcg (micrograms) of alcohol per 100-ml (millilitres) of breath
Urine: 107 mg (milligrams) of alcohol per 100-ml (millilitres) of urine

The Scottish limit for driving is

Blood: 50 mg (milligrams) of alcohol per 100-ml (millilitres) of blood
Breath: 22 mcg (micrograms) of alcohol per 100-ml (millilitres) of breath
Urine: 67 mg (milligrams) of alcohol per 100-ml (millilitres of urine

> Note: What are the limits in your country or company?

Alcohol testing procedure (SOP no.)

(a) The employee attends a suitable location, where the breath test is to be administered using the selected company electronic breath-alcohol testing device.

(b) The individual may be accompanied by a witness (e.g. union representative or if required nominated colleague not implicated in the reason for the test).

(c) The testing procedure is explained to the individual.

(d) The employee is then required to sign a Consent Form regarding this impending test.

(e) If an individual refuses to give a breath specimen or subsequently repeatedly obstructs the collection of a correct specimen the individual is informed that such a refusal or obstruction is a failure to comply with this policy and as such will invoke the company disciplinary procedure, which may lead to summary dismissal.

(f) The breath test is administered according to the instructions.

(g) The donor should not smoke or have had anything to eat or drink for 20 minutes prior to the test.

(h) If the first test is negative (no reading) a second test is not required.

(i) If the breath test shows a reading greater than 0 or 35 micrograms (using the electronic device), then the individual is asked to wait 20 minutes, at which time a second breath test is administered.

(j) The results of the second breath test are taken to be definitive.

(k) If the second test reading is higher than the first but below the 35-microgram cut-off this indicates the donor may have been drinking recently, as it appears the breath alcohol level is rising. The donor should be questioned about his or her recent drinking.

(l) If the second test reading is lower than the 35-microgram cut-off level then the donor's breath alcohol level is falling, which indicates that the donor may have been drinking heavily some time prior to the test and should be questioned accordingly.

(m) If the second test is positive, above 35 micrograms, then the individual will be suspended awaiting a disciplinary hearing. The employee will be escorted off the premises. Employees will be advised they should not drive their own vehicle and that alternative travel arrangements should be made. If they choose to drive the vehicle, then the police will be informed immediately.

(n) Any time lost through such precautionary suspension will be with pay.

Normal earnings will be paid for any scheduled time lost at work. (Optional.)

1. Drug testing procedure

Introduction

There are different methods for testing for drugs in the body. Testing for drug misuse depends on the collection of oral fluid, urine, hair or fingernail clipping samples for analysis which can be achieved by the use of a portable testing kit for preliminary screening, or the sample can be sent to a toxicology using a back to laboratory (BTL) kit for analysis.

To dispel any doubts over the validity of the testing methods, the company uses methods of testing that are currently recognized throughout the industry. The company can use disposable and laboratory drug testing kits for analysis. A UKAS-accredited analytical laboratory is always used for detailed analysis and confirmation of samples. The company recognizes that these methods are the current best practices and best available technology with which to implement the policy.

Drug testing procedures involve up to five stages depending on whether a positive result is obtained. All are strictly controlled by a process referred to as 'chain of custody'. The stages involved are summarized here:

1. Sample collection
2. Adulteration testing (urine only)
3. Preliminary screening
4. Confirmatory analysis
5. Reporting of results. (Consideration can be given to a Medical Review Officer (MRO) input at this stage.)

Drug/substance misuse sample collection information

Chain of custody is the name given to the procedures that are employed to ensure that a sample travels in an intact and secure manner from the donor to the laboratory and all the way through the laboratory process up to, and including, the reporting of the laboratory results and possible medical review.

The individual will be asked to consent and donate a sample of urine or oral fluid for screening using the procedures for sample collection given by the manufacturer and/or the analytical laboratory.

The donor will witness the sample collection and also the record keeping and identification procedure for the sample. This is the only stage of the procedure that the donor will witness, so it is important that the collection is undertaken properly and under the correct supervision.

An appointed collection service as nominated by the company may be called to undertake the procedure.

Adulteration testing for urinalysis only

The whole procedure will be carefully witnessed to prevent adulteration or substitution of other substances by the donor. The donor's sample is taken labelled and placed in a container with a tamper-evident seal for shipment to the testing laboratory. The urine and oral fluid specimen is divided and placed in two containers, which are uniquely labelled and sealed with tamper-evident seals. The urine remaining in the collection cup will be tested immediately for adulteration by inspection of colour, temperature, etc.

Note: If a urine sample cannot be provided by the donor within 3 hours or prior to the end of the employee's shift then an oral fluid sample will be taken.

Adulteration testing of oral fluid

When employees are selected for oral fluid testing no adulteration tests are required. The donor should, however, have abstained from chewing gum, eating, drinking and smoking for at least 10 minutes prior to the test being administered. Please refer to collection device and collection documentation for further information.

Hair samples

Hair samples are sent for laboratory analysis only. Negative results are generally reported within 24 hours of receipt at the laboratory. Positive samples will be examined via a variety of additional processes and those results will be sent to the company within a maximum of 3 working days. No adulteration tests are required for hair analysis. The only consideration necessary for the submission of a hair sample is the removal of hair extensions.

Confirmatory analysis

The laboratory will first ensure that the samples have not been tampered with to confirm the chain of custody. The sample container is then opened for laboratory preliminary analysis to exclude adulteration and then the sample is subject to extensive analysis to screen for the range of drugs using immunoassay techniques. In the event the urine collection is an instant indication for the presence of selected drug metabolites then the sample may go straight to the confirmation process selected by the company.

If the analytical laboratory immunoassay tests prove positive, then specific methods are used to determine the sample contents (these being gas or liquid chromatography and mass spectrometry). These methods are used as part of the confirmatory analysis procedure.

Toxicology and reporting of results

All stages of the analysis are carefully monitored by analytical laboratory toxicologists. Once the results are known they may be reported to a laboratory toxicologist who will interpret the results of the analysis, which will subsequently and confidentially be reported to the relevant company manager for company procedures to be completed.

2. Drug testing collection procedure (SOP no.   )

(a) The employee is informed that they have been selected to be tested for drugs and the testing procedure will be explained to the individual.

(b) The individual attends a suitable location where the samples are to be collected.

(c) The individual may be accompanied by a witness (e.g. relevant union representative or if required nominated colleague not connected with the reason for the test).

(d) The donor's ID will need to be made known and confirmed to the collector.

(e) The individual is then required to sign a Consent Form regarding this impending test.

(f) The donor will be asked if they are taking any prescribed medication and provide proof by way of a prescription. The donor will also be asked if they take illegal substances on an occasional or regular basis and when they last took such a substance.

(g) The donor will be allowed to select the appropriate test device from at least five or more sealed devices.

(h) The collector and donor will check that the collection device is in date and packaging is not damaged.

(i) If a point of care device (instant result) is initially being used and it shows a negative result, then that result is recorded onto the Client Collection Form (CCF), which is a contemporaneous record of events. If the sample is a presumptive positive, then a back to laboratory (BTL) sample will be collected using a different device but selected as before from a sealed in-date batch. In the case of a urine collection, a sample of the original urine will be decanted into a BTL kit. For a saliva sample, a second BTL kit will be used and the original point of care device retained or photographed.

(j) The laboratory sample is taken from the donor by the competent person. A designated collection service may also be called for assistance in sample collection

(k) With regard to urine, the sample will be examined by various methods to ensure that adulteration has not occurred.

(l) If ascertained that adulteration has occurred, then this will constitute a breach of the company's disciplinary procedure up to and including dismissal.

(m) If an individual refuses to give a urine, oral fluid or hair sample the individual is informed that such a refusal is a failure to comply with this policy and, as such, will invoke the company's disciplinary procedure. The same applies at any time when consent is withdrawn during the collection process.

(n) Once the collection is complete the donor and the collector will ensure that all signatures, dates and other marks are complete before the sample is sealed in its evidence bag in the presence of all concerned.

(o) The donor will then be informed of the company's process for the delivery of a sample being sent for analysis. This may include overnight storage and safe custody of the sample.

(p) For point of care testing devices which provide an instant presumptive positive or the donor confesses to the misuse of substances, the donor may be required to be interviewed under the company's guidelines for investigative and disciplinary action. The sample collection process must be completed first.

(q) If the analytical laboratory result is subsequently negative (this may take up to 5 days for verification) and depending on the outcome of the internal investigation the individual will then be asked to sign a record, and will be free to return to work. The company may reimburse payment for the period of suspension

(r) If the analytical laboratory result is positive, then the individual will continue to be suspended with pay while awaiting a disciplinary investigation. A copy of the sample result must be given to the individual within 72 hours of it being received by the company.

Company code of conduct

To comply with the company's Substance Misuse Policy, all employees should

(a) Be aware of their fiduciary duty to be fit for work.
(b) Be aware of their own tolerance to intoxicating liquor.
(c) Be aware of drinking guidelines (e.g. a person's body rids itself of one unit of alcohol per hour).
(d) Be aware of their own shift patterns and regulate their drinking habits accordingly.
(e) Comply with the need to be fit for work and driving to work under a variety of legislations.

Also, employees should not

(a) Have the smell of intoxicating liquor on their breath while on duty. This would especially apply where face-to-face contact with customers and the general public is involved.

(b) Report for work if they have any doubt about their fitness.
(c) Drink alcohol during meal breaks/split shifts unless it is part of a business meeting.
(d) Drive any company vehicle after taking intoxicating liquor, illegal drugs, prescribed medicines or other substances which may affect their legal capacity to drive.
(e) Be in possession of or traffic or under the influence of illegal drugs/substances.

All employees must

(a) Inform any medical practitioner or pharmacist dispensing medicine that they need to understand any side effects of the medication that may impact the user's ability to conduct their contracted job description. There are usually alternative medications available that will not impair your ability to work.
(b) Check whether any medication that they are currently taking will affect their capacity to safely and effectively undertake the duties of their post or change of duty requested of them.
(c) Inform senior management of the company of any prescribed treatments or over-the-counter (OTC) treatments they are currently taking that will or are affecting their capacity to safely execute any reasonable request made of them.

Background information

The Substance and Alcohol Misuse Policy and Programme Of Testing covers all types of substance and alcohol misuse. This includes the misuse of substances which are categorized as illegal drugs, legal drugs and medicines/restricted drugs and other substances which come to the notice of the company.

1. Illegal drugs

These can be grouped into three categories: Depressants, Stimulants and Hallucinogens. These substances, termed 'controlled drugs' under the Misuse of Drugs Act 1971, are classified as either Class A, B or C (as defined in Schedule 2 of the Act).

1.1 Depressants

Opiates such as heroin, morphine and opium are in this category and are sniffed, swallowed, smoked or injected. These drugs are also classed as narcotics and as Class A. Use of these drugs can lead to increased tolerance, resulting in both physical and psychological dependency. Sustained use of these substances can cause a user to centre their lifestyle around the drug's procurement and use.

Cannabis is usually smoked or eaten and short-term effects can lead to loss of concentration and slowed reactions leading to impaired work performance. Longer-term effects can result in psychological dependence, respiratory problems and lung cancer.

1.2 Stimulants

Amphetamines are sniffed, swallowed or injected. These increase pulse rate and blood pressure. Use can result in anxiety and panic and increasing risk of both emotional and physical dependence with increasing use. Chronic effects can also lead to a reduced resistance to infection and a loss of appetite leading to weight loss.

Cocaine, and its derivatives, is either sniffed, smoked or injected. Use can lead to psychosis and delusions. Repeated use can lead to a high risk of dependence. Extreme effects can be encountered when using cocaine when prepared as crack such as heart failure or heart attack.

1.3 Hallucinogens

These can include lysergic acid diethylamide (LSD) and hallucinogenic amphetamines (MDMA, Ecstasy). These drugs are generally ingested, and effects can range from anxiety and panic to extreme perceptual disorders leading to reckless behaviour.

Phencyclidine (PCP, angel dust) can be sniffed or smoked and can lead to irregular breathing, hallucinations in the short term and severe depression and psychosis coupled with violent behaviour.

2. Legal drugs

2.1 Prescribed medications

These are legally available only on medical prescription through a medical practitioner to a named patient. Many prescribed medications are Class A, B or C drugs under the Misuse of Drugs Act. If you are in possession of these medications and do not have or have not been prescribed them you are committing an offence under the Misuse of Drugs Act relevant to the class of drug; e.g. tramadol is a Class C drug, Codeine is a Class B drug, and methadone is a Class A drug.

Examples of medicines/prescribed drugs can be tranquillizers such as benzodiazepines (e.g. temazepam, Valium (diazepam), Librium, Ativan, Serenid, Normison), which can be swallowed or injected. These drugs have severe risks of both physical and psychological dependence. Other examples can be antidepressants, sleeping pills and some medicines such as remedies for coughs and colds.

2.2 Solvent misuse

Solvents are volatile substances that can include cigarette lighter fluids (and associated hydrocarbons), cleaning fluids, adhesives and aerosol preparations. Misuse of these items can lead to severe intoxication and disorientation with increasing risk of heart and brain damage with increasing use. All solvent misuse is now covered under the Psychoactive Substances Act and all relevant penalties apply.

3. Alcohol

All intoxicating liquors containing alcohol such as beer, wine and spirits, including so-called 'low alcohol' products, are included in this category.

Alcohol is absorbed into the bloodstream and is carried to all parts of the body including the brain. It affects the part of the brain which controls judgement and physical co-ordination. Excessive and regular consumption can result in dependency and can lead to the medical condition of alcoholism based on the tolerance to the alcohol and the inability by the individual to limit intake. Nausea and vomiting can occur from an excess of alcohol and very large doses can lead to poisoning or death from suffocation.

Chronic effects of heavy, sustained use of alcoholic products can lead to alcoholic hepatitis, cirrhosis of the liver, cancer and other liver diseases.

The risks of other diseases such as coronary heart disease, stroke and high blood pressure are also compounded by high usage. Alcoholics face a higher risk of developing stomach complaints such as peptic ulcers as well as suffering from psychological conditions such as anxiety, depression and irreversible mental deterioration.

4. Psychoactive substances (what were known as 'legal highs', bath salts, synthetic substances)

Psychoactive substances were previously known as 'legal highs' and are manufactured as synthetic products to provide reactions similar to those experienced by illegal drugs and other substances. Psychoactive substances contain a wide variety of compounds from weed killers to illegal drugs. To avoid prosecution from human abuse, packaging is marked 'Not fit for human consumption' or 'plant food'. The use of these psychoactive substances is extremely dangerous and has led to the deaths of numerous people. Furthermore, any combination of illegal drugs, prescribed medicines and/or alcohol can and does lead to numerous deaths annually in the UK and globally.

UK meaning of 'psychoactive substance' etc.

(1) In this Act 'psychoactive substance' means any substance which
    (a) is capable of producing a psychoactive effect in a person who consumes it,
    and
    (b) is not an exempted substance (see Section 3).
(2) For the purposes of this Act a substance produces a psychoactive effect in a person if, by stimulating or depressing the person's central nervous system, it affects the person's mental functioning or emotional state; and references to a substance's psychoactive effects are to be read accordingly.
(3) For the purposes of this Act a person consumes a substance if the person causes or allows the substance, or fumes given off by the substance, to enter the person's body in any way.

Management of drug/alcohol incident report (SOP no.)

Record/assessment of a situation where an employee is reported as suspected of being under the influence of drugs and or alcohol at work.

Name of employee/contractor _____

DOB _____ **Time** _____

Position _____ **Location** _____

Name of person reporting the situation _____

Position _____

Reason for the report (What has happened? What has been observed?)

_____

_____

_____

_____

_____

_____

_____

_____

_____

Signature of person reporting _____

Date _____

Time _____

Manager's assessment of the situation

The above named employee has been reported to me as outlined above and I have made the following assessment.

The employee/contractor:

1. Smells of intoxicating liquor * / slurring speech * .... Yes/No

2. Has a change in normal behaviour .... Yes/No

(Brief detail) _____

_____

3. Has difficulty with concentration .... Yes/No

4. Eyes appear large and staring .... Yes/No

5. Appears to be euphoric*/ drowsy*/ depressed .... Yes/No

6. Has been involved in an incident*/accident* ....…... Yes/No

(*Circle appropriate responses.)

(Brief detail) _____

_____

7. There is evidence of alcohol use at work ....…............. Yes/No

8. Drug paraphernalia has been found at his/her workplace .... Yes/No

(Provide detail of what was found and where, e.g. foil, tins, drugs, alcohol, etc.)

_____

_____

_____

_____

Who was the incident reported to/by?

Name: _____ Position: _____

Date: _____ Time: _____

Action taken by manager: _____

_____

_____

_____

_____

_____

_____

Alcohol breath test carried out   Yes / No   1st Reading ____ 2nd Reading ____

Drug screening carried out   Yes / No   Result _____

Hair* Urine* Saliva*   Point of care device*   Laboratory*

(*Circle appropriate response.)

Name of manager: _____

Signature of manager: _____ Date: _____

Additional comments _____

_____

_____

_____

_____

Template Substance and Alcohol Misuse Policy (SAMP) acknowledgement

My signature below acknowledges that I have been informed of the Company's Substance and Alcohol Misuse Policy (SAMP), Programme Of Testing (POT) and Employee Assistance Programme (EAP).

I have received a copy of the SAMP memorandum, and I have been offered an opportunity to review the Company's Substance Misuse Testing Policy and Procedures.

Furthermore, I understand that employee testing is a condition of continued employment. I agree to comply with the rules and regulations as described in the SAMP and understand that failure to do so may lead to disciplinary action being taken against me up to and including dismissal.

I can confirm that I am not currently prescribed any drug treatment medication which has a statutory requirement for me to declare to DVLA that may result in my driving license being suspended or removed.

I will comply with all statutory demands that require me to inform my employer and DVLA that my treatment, medical condition, misuse of drugs or prescribed medication requires that I surrender my driving licence or subject myself to assessment in order to keep my driving licence.

Applicant name (print):

Applicant signature:

Date:

Witness name (print):

Witness signature:

Date:

Template authorization for release of information

I hereby authorize any drug testing laboratory designated by the Company to keep and process my information and to release to the Company or its designated agents the results of the laboratory test to which I have consented for the purpose of determining the presence of drugs or alcohol in my body.

I expressly understand and agree that the Company will review the results of these tests in connection with making a decision concerning my application for employment and/or a decision concerning my continuing employment at the Company.

Other than for the purpose of making a determination concerning my application for employment and/or a decision concerning my continued employment at the Company, I understand that the Company shall not use or further disclose any information released pursuant to this authorization unless further expressly authorized by me or unless such disclosure is required by law but within General Data Protection Regulations.

This authorization shall become effective immediately and remain in effect until (specify…..). I understand that I have the right to receive a copy of this authorization upon request.

Print name:

Signature:

Date:

Witness print name:

Witness signature:

Date:

Template employee consent and release from liability

I understand that the Company has a policy against the possession, use, sale or transfer of illegal drugs by its employees. I further understand that the Company is committed to a substance- and alcohol-free workforce and that employee substance and alcohol testing is one method of implementing that policy.

I acknowledge that I have or can be provided an opportunity to seek intervention through the company-sponsored Employee Assistance Program. I further acknowledge that I have previously received a copy of the Drug Testing Policy Memorandum, and I have been offered an opportunity to review the Company's Drug and Alcohol Testing Policies and Procedures. I understand that employee testing is a condition of continued employment.

I hereby consent to the taking of my hair/fingernail clippings/urine/oral fluid/breath alcohol or hair alcohol samples by the Company or its agents and to the testing of such samples by any such drug testing laboratory (the 'laboratory') designated by the Company. I hereby further consent to the laboratory holding and processing my details and the release of the drug test results from the laboratory to agents of the Company and the Company itself.

I do hereby release the laboratory, its officers, employees, agents and representatives, from any and all liabilities arising from the authorized release or use of the information contained in my test result for employment purposes.

I release and discharge the Company, its officers and agents, from any claim or liability arising from the use of such tests for any decisions concerning employment made by the Company based, in whole or in part, upon the results of such a test. Should the test results be confirmed to be positive, and no acceptable explanation is provided, I will be subject to disciplinary action, which may include immediate termination.

Employee print name:

Employee signature:

Date:

Witness name (print):

Witness signature:

Chapter summary

This chapter outlines the basic minimum requirements of a phased or modular approach to the whole company package of substance and alcohol misuse control and countermeasure. It further highlights other areas which also need careful consideration into other situations of T&Cs of employment, cross-reference to other policies, staff handbooks or integrity programmes and more.

In larger companies or a company with multiple sites I would, as stated, advise the creation of a committee to build and develop the whole programme. It is too much for one person, with other duties, to research, manage and implement the range of knowledge required for a robust SAMP and all that goes with it.

The policy document should be the only document challenged or taken to litigation. Within the SAMP and POT Administration Manual there are SOPs that can be varied with your provider's own documentation and processes to reflect your chosen test mediums or analytical services. The Administration Manual can also hold other local or company-specific documents you deem fit to develop for the benefit of your company's SAMP, POT, EAP, etc.

Remember, here at Hall & Angus we review our clients' SAMP whenever new legislation comes to notice, employment law changes or new scientific developments come to notice that require the SAMP to be updated. IN ANY EVENT, we review the client SAMP every 6 months; we do not set it and forget it.

Do

1. Have a robust SAMP, POT and EAP in place whether you intend to test or not.
2. At the start of a Programme of Testing announce an amnesty period for consultation with staff and the training of managers.
3. Announce when the start date of testing will be or is available for introduction.
4. Make a fair presentation to your insurer about the strength of your SAMP, POT and EAP.
5. Make sure you have set your company standards in any SAMP and who they apply to under which circumstances.

6. Make sure you have highlighted in the SAMP the consequences of breaching those standards.
7. Integrate the SAMP into other documents and policies where appropriate.
8. Create an EAP for immediate initiation after the announcement of the start of the amnesty period.
9. Identify to the workplace who the Implementation Committee are and the route for Q&A's.
10. Conduct shift briefings about how the SAMP, POT and EAP will be applied or made available.
11. Introduce poster campaigns.
12. Examine your T&Cs of employment and how they integrate with your SAMP.
13. Remove all general information and non-policy information into a SAMP, POT and EAP administration manual.
14. Train your managers and leaders in how to manage the SAMP, POT and EAP.
15. Ensure your SAMP, POT and EAP are legally defensible.
16. Make sure every request for testing or enrolment into an EAP is done with consent, and the consent is explained and documented.

Do not

1. Think you can start testing immediately after you make a decision to do so or have a need to.
2. Go it alone because you will likely fail. Locate an expert service provider and let them drive the development with your support.
3. Dismiss employees as a result of using a screening device whether for drugs or alcohol.
4. Have a SAMP that is either too verbose so you have to defend all of its content or so brief that it does not protect the company or its employees.
5. Fill the SAMP with limited legislations. The legislations you leave out will be just as important as the ones you put in. Restrict the mention of legislations to the need of the company to comply with a variety of civil and criminal legislations.
6. Leave your T&Cs of employment exposed with regard to SAMP, POT and EAP compliance with statutory requirements.

7. Put general information into the SAMP. It is unenforceable and has no part to play in any subsequent disciplinary action.
8. Take consent for granted. Under GDPR you must have a written consent and an understanding that the person consenting knows what they are consenting to.
9. Expect that random testing using a non-evidential test device that often fails is a deterrent in the workplace. Your employees will research your programme and your test mediums. Be sure they are robust; that is the deterrent.

The workplace

Employee Assistance Programme

Introduction

Already outlined in Chapters 1–3 and repeated in other chapters is the need for a *managed* workplace Employee Assistance Programme (EAP). Many companies have such programmes in place that cover multiple situations in addition to substance and alcohol misuse. There are, however, a wide range of civil and criminal legislations that are applied to substance and alcohol misuse, and the company has to risk assess and manage them all alongside their insurance obligations and corporate governance.

The EAP is *the* most effective methodology to manage workplace substance and alcohol misuse situations within the confines of employment law for existing employees. Its place within and alongside the Substance and Alcohol Misuse Policy (SAMP) and Programme Of Testing (POT) is the final part of the three-pronged delivery to a robust proactive policy and a company's approach to managing the very complicated subject of substance and alcohol misuse across employment law and those criminal and civil legislations which keep appearing on the horizon of treatment and management.

In the very early stages of developing the company's approach to the management of substance and alcohol misuse in the workplace, there is a need to very quickly develop and provide a mechanism to manage those staff who have underlying issues around substance and alcohol misuse/dependency.

In Phase 1, the initial companywide announcement, the offer of self-referring an issue is made available, especially during the amnesty period. However, any employee can self-refer any substance or alcohol issues at any time during their employment. The announcement of the introduction of a companywide SAMP and POT will instil fear into those staff who have to this point gone unnoticed or hidden within the workforce and who have until now:

- Casually misused substances and continue to use/misuse substances in their private lives.
- Self-medicated a problem they did not want exposed.
- Had a chronic misuse issue of illegal or legal substances.
- Developed a specific substance dependency, whether illegal or legal substances.
- Developed other comorbidities around substance misuse that have an additional impact on their mental and physical wellbeing.
- Not had the opportunity to enrol into a confidential mechanism for treatment/assessment in or away from the workplace.
- Not trusted the company's existing provision or ability to deliver an appropriate and proportionate intervention or solution of their problem.
- Not been required to or felt the need to self-refer an issue until the announcement of a company testing programme.

The physical and mental wellbeing of any employee and a collective workforce is paramount to the company and the day-to-day operations of its business, whether local, national or global. Working with the right provider will allow you to *fast track* specialist interventions that can deal with the mental and physical impact of substance and alcohol misuse issues, as well as other comorbidities or unmet needs that often exist or come to notice. Existing UK NHS waiting lists for interventions or other support mechanisms are varied across the UK and can take months before an initial assessment is conducted. The facts that a person is in employment, receiving a wage and has a home to go to are often barriers to immediate NHS or other rehabilitation prequalifications for a rapid intervention.

Before you start the EAP process

Before you start the process of offering a full EAP support package there is always the need to identify the nature and extent of the problem you are dealing with. There is also a need to consider two statutory requirements for the UK:

1. The employee's statutory duty to report their substance misuse/dependency to the Driver and Vehicle Licensing Agency (DVLA) if they are a

licence holder (conditions apply) or licence applicant. It is for DVLA to take any action regarding the employee's fitness to hold a licence. The employer cannot report this need; it is a self-referring requirement of the licence holder only.

> Note: Be aware of your insurance risk/obligations, especially where an employee is required to drive a company vehicle on a public road, as well as considerations around their specific position and activities within the company. You should ask a range of questions at pre-employment that are similar to DVLA declarations, especially around the need to drive on behalf of the company. What are the rules in your country?

2. The employer's duty to comply with safeguarding issues of those employees who have been identified as regular or chronic substance misusers and have children who may or may not be at risk, especially with regard to the risk of significant harm. There is a need to inform social services of situations where children may be at risk. It is for social services to decide what action is taken thereafter.

> Note: Be sure that you as an employer or manager have a clear conscience and have complied with your legal duty. What are the safeguarding regulations and requirements in your country? For the UK see below.

Children Act 1989 Section 47 – Duty to Investigate

Where there is reasonable cause to suspect that a child is suffering, or likely to suffer, *significant harm*, the local authority is required under s47 of the Children Act 1989 to make enquiries, to enable it to decide whether it should take any action to safeguard and promote the welfare of the child.

The concept of significant harm within the Children Act 1989: www.nspcc. org.uk

Some children are in need because they are suffering, or likely to suffer, significant harm as a result of parental/carer/family abuse or neglect. The Children Act 1989 introduced the concept of significant harm as the threshold that justifies *compulsory* intervention in family life in the best interests of children and gives local authorities a duty to make enquiries to decide whether they should take action to safeguard or promote the welfare of a child who is suffering, or likely to suffer, significant harm.

There are no absolute criteria on which to rely when judging what constitutes significant harm. Consideration of the severity of ill treatment may include the degree and the extent of physical harm; the duration and frequency of abuse and neglect; the extent of premeditation; and the presence or degree of threat, coercion, sadism and bizarre or unusual elements. Each of these elements has been associated with more severe effects on the child and/or relatively greater difficulty in helping the child overcome the adverse impact of the maltreatment.

Sometimes, a single traumatic event may constitute significant harm, for example, a violent assault, suffocation or poisoning. More often, significant harm is a compilation of significant events, both acute and long-standing, which interrupt, change or damage the child's physical and psychological development. Some children live in family and social circumstances where their health and development are neglected. For them, it is the corrosiveness of long-term emotional, physical or sexual abuse that causes impairment to the extent of constituting significant harm. In each case, it is necessary to consider any maltreatment alongside the child's own assessment of his or her safety and welfare, the family's strengths and supports, as well as an assessment of the likelihood and capacity for change and improvements in parenting and the care of children and young people.

To understand and identify significant harm, it is necessary to consider:

- The nature of harm, in terms of maltreatment or failure to provide adequate care.
- The impact on the child's health and development.
- The child's development within the context of their family and wider environment.

- Any special needs, such as a medical condition, communication impairment or disability, that may affect the child's development and care within the family.
- The capacity of parents to meet the child's needs adequately.
- The wider and environmental family context.

The start of the EAP

The way to begin the EAP process with regard to substance and or alcohol misuse/abuse is to take a wide-window drug sample from the employee: cut head hair, body hair or, as a last resort, fingernail clippings. The wide-window test works on the basis that drugs stay in hair/fingernail clippings reasonably permanently and are proportionate to use for regular users. You do not rehabilitate use of all drugs the same way; titration from large doses down to lower doses takes time. Also take in tandem with the wide-window test a narrow-window test to examine the then and there scenario of substance misuse habits of the employee, if any are admitted or exist.

Document your assessment, giving the employee ample opportunity to tell you the full truth of the situation. Remind them that a wide-window test will detect anything taken during that wide-window period. An EAP requires the employee to be totally honest. It also requires that the employer ask the right questions around the employee's situation and working history. Lying at the start of an EAP is a measure of the employee's lack of commitment to it.

In addition, if the employee is actually shown to be a cocktail substance misuser in the regular to chaotic misuse category, then their rehabilitation may be protracted and complicated beyond the employee's continued suitability for employment. So, for EAP protocols, start with a hair analysis and rely in the first place on the quantitative and qualitative analysis results from the laboratory and combine them with any interview/admission content from the donor.

Where the workplace culture map (Chapter 6) identifies the negatives and positives within a range of subjects across all company operations, the EAP deals with a range of elements within the treatment and management of the employee. Just like the four-phased implementation of the SAMP there is a need for the EAP to be based on a four-phased approach throughout any employee intervention/support package.

Phases

Once the sample results have been analysed, the company needs to make a decision as to how far it can practicably be prepared to go in the support of the individual employee's potential and bespoke treatment programme. There is a need to give anyone with a substance misuse issue support over a period of time and following a set process, outlined below. This does not apply to those employees who do not meet the enrolment criteria or who because of other issues are excluded from the programme. Each employee enroled must consent to enrolment; see the template consent form that follows. Each employee will have different needs from the *recovery-oriented intervention*; the phases that follow are the minimum application for a fair assessment and employee support package.

1. The examination of the employee's relevant *Treatment History*.
2. The identification of any *Unmet Needs*, declared or otherwise
3. The identification of a *Treatment Profile(s)*.
4. The identification of and management towards a *Treatment Outcome*.

Phase 1. The treatment history. This will require that the employee provide consent for the company or its appointed agent to have access to the employee's *relevant* medical history via their GP records – not the whole medical history, just the area relevant to the identified issue(s). The GP or a referral from the GP may be the company's chosen agent. The GP should be given a copy of the company's EAP consent document so that they can become an integral part of the reporting and treatment process that will ultimately decide if the employee is fit for work and the development and introduction of Phase 2, 3 and 4 interventions. At this stage, the company will be in the possession of the hair analysis result and should have already spent time with the employee to fact find and risk assess the expectation of both the employee and the company. It is for the employee to keep their GP in the loop. Employees can be and often are placed on UK statutory sick pay during this stage if they cannot be allowed into the workplace. *What is available in your country with regard to this facility?*

Phase 2. The identification of any unmet needs. This will require a considered approach to the questioning of the employee, a review of the employee's relevant clinical history and a close examination of the toxicology report(s).

As with any dependency issues the individual may have gone into denial and not told their GP of their true situation in or away from the workplace. The GP has, just as the employer does, a need to ask the right questions at the right time under the right circumstances. Sadly, in the current UK climate, many who attend GP surgeries are under a time restriction imposed by the surgery during their visit. They do not always see the same GP, resort to self-medication using black market medications or illegal substances or visit multiple online doctors to accumulate multiple medications above and beyond a normal prescription or treatment profile. In the event this is the case, just like the above, the employee should keep the GP in the loop. Too many people take the depressant drug 'alcohol' to manage their depression. This needs to change by better education and poster campaigns in the workplace.

Phase 3. The identification of a treatment profile(s). The treatment profile(s) will be dictated by a number of elements:

• The single or multiple illnesses or symptoms identified and the honesty/integrity of the employee
• The result of any toxicology report
• An agreed time frame for treatment in line with the SAMP, terms and conditions (T&Cs) of employment or any other mitigating factor(s) identified by the company
• The employee's commitment to the treatment profile and notification to the GP
• The employer's commitment to the treatment profile and outcome

Phase 4. The identification of a treatment outcome. The treatment outcome, like the treatment profile, will have a number of elements which will revolve around the employees:

1. Fitness for a phased return to work
2. Fitness for a full return to work
3. Not fit for return to their original position, but fit for another position, a reasonable adjustment, if available
4. Not fit for any return to work to any position within the company

The EAP throughout each of its phases and the elements contained within them requires the company to commit to the programme and set clear and unambiguous compliance standards that have enrolment, exclusion and removal criteria.

The goal of the company is to develop a process that allows the employee as much latitude to fulfil what can be a tremendous life adjustment without becoming an unresolved problem to themselves, their family and their company.

The goal of the EAP is to provide a *recovery-oriented* treatment package that benefits the employer and the employee across their workplace experience and including, where appropriate, their family/life experience. It also helps justify any decisions taken in relation to the employee.

The goal of the employee throughout all aspects of the EAP is the requirement to consent to the intervention and comply with treatment recommendations, expert advice offered and above all to be totally honest with themselves, the employer and their treatment provider throughout the programme.

Where necessary the employee may have to concede to a reasonable role adjustment, with any relevant drop in pay during treatment if they are not suspended. In every situation there is a need to manage any risk to the company and the employee within a risk assessment at every stage. Remember, there is also a need for the company to comply with its operational risk as outlined to the company's insurance provider as well as the need to comply with a wide range of criminal and civil legislations, including statutory requirements that can be applied in a variety of situations. While it is not your duty to report an employee's substance misuse to DVLA, you can and should prevent them from driving a company vehicle on a public road until they have reported to DVLA and indicated action has been taken that you can keep in the employee's personnel file. This is critical when it comes to any action taken against the company via criminal or civil proceedings that involve that person and the company has to justify what steps they have taken to protect the employee, the public and the business. You may also find that if you take the wrong action it will compromise your insurance obligations.

The process outlined above can also cover rehabilitation for misuse of prescribed medications as well as illegal substances. The difference between the two is that the legally prescribed substances can have short-, medium- or long-term applications and side effects. Liaise with your provider to assess the nature of prescribed medication from a GP that impacts the company with role-related issues that prohibit the employee's *Fiduciary Duty* to be *Fit for Work*. Remember, many employees take regular medications to be fit for work. Make sure you have an open and confidential route to referring those issues within the company and the employee's concerns. Sadly, many employees who take drugs to be fit for work can actually be rendered unfit for work due to the debilitating side effects of some prescribed medications.

To assist the employer and the employee Hall & Angus have designed the following template document to record, consent and compliance across a range of situations as explained in this chapter. At the end of the document are the exclusion and removal criteria, and these must be read and understood before the employee signs the consent to comply with the conditions of the company-sponsored EAP. The witness in particular should go through all aspects of the document with the employee to make sure they fully understand the ramifications of failing, obstructing or rescinding any consent during the course of the EAP. The original copy of the document should be kept on the employee's personnel file. Controlled copies can be produced for delivery to the employee's GP or other specialist clinicians with the consent of the employee.

As with all operational documents they should come under the control of any company accreditation system applied, such as the International Organization for Standardization (ISO), General Data Protection Regulation (GDPR), etc. All such documents can be kept apart from the SAMP and POT Administration Manual but it is a good idea to have reference copies available in the manual.

Hall & Angus Template Document

The Company

Consent Document for an EAP Programme (SOP no.)

I...employee no.................................wish to self-refer into the company employee assistance programme. I declare that the issues I have confidentially outlined to the HR department are having an impact on my mental/physical/general wellbeing. I am aware of the inclusion, removal and exclusion criteria (overleaf), the implications of which have been explained to me.

I am prepared to submit to a recovery-oriented treatment programme supported by clinical interventions where necessary that are appointed from within the company programme. I will further notify my GP of my enrolment into the EAP and ask that they support the programme provider and my employer with any requested medical records or information.

I will support the company and its treatment providers in the provision of my past and current treatment history and respond to any identified unmet need that may require additional support.

I am aware that my current role may need to be changed to facilitate a reasonable adjustment while I am enrolled in the company EAP.

I am prepared to submit to regular treatment effectiveness reviews while on the EAP and am aware that any unqualified obstruction or refusal to meet their needs can result in removal from the EAP programme to the detriment of my position within the company up to and including dismissal.

Signed.. Date............................

Print name.. Position.......................

Witnessed.. Date............................

Print name.. Position.......................

(See over for enrolment, exclusion and removal criteria before signing.)

Enrolment/exclusion criteria:
The manner of referral may not be appropriate under the circumstances of the need to refer, e.g.,

- *Circumstances that lead to the self-referral were preceded by a criminal act or act of gross misconduct within the company (company decision)*
- *Where substance misuse was discovered prior to self-referral, post-test, etc.*
- *Where the company disciplinary process has already been activated*
- *Where the problem referred was already a statutory requirement under the Road Traffic Act (DVLA) or part of an existing treatment programme which has statutory requirements attached to it*
- *Employee refuses to enrol in the programme when an issue has been identified*

Removal criteria
The removal criteria may be activated when a person who is enrolled in the company EAP:

- *Obstructs, in whole or in part of the EAP treatment/intervention requirements*
- *Fails to attend without reasonable cause any treatment sessions or specialist interventions*
- *After due consideration it is decided that recovery is unlikely*
- *Relapses to a previous reason to enrol into the programme*
- *Leaves the company*
- *Fails without reasonable cause to adhere to GP or programme provider's advice and guidance*

Note: The Company reserves the right to add to or remove any of the above criteria as and when the need arises or the nature of civil or criminal legislations changes.

Monitoring of employees post-EAP

Depending on the report(s) of the treatment provider and the employee's GP and in agreement with the employee certain situations will require periodic monitoring for an agreed period of time. This may be up to 2 years in duration after the EAP has been satisfactorily completed. This is one of the few areas where I agree with the need for a random workplace testing protocol but only using back to laboratory analysis.

Continued monitoring is required for some dependencies and forms part of a complete treatment and recovery-oriented programme designed for the benefit of the employee and the company.

Example

Where an employee who has been a substance misuser/dependent and continues to be rehabilitated, there is a need, for the benefit of the employee and the company, to continue random testing protocols to ensure that the employee does not relapse or is supported in a continued recovery programme, which is another direct social return on investment (SROI) for society from an employer initiative.

The company will always reserve the right to employ a variety of methods to monitor employees who are enrolled in the company EAP. Where paid absence is available, the company should remind those who are enrolled in the EAP that they continue to be employees of the company while absent from the workplace. Accordingly, paid absence requires that the T&Cs of the employee's contract of employment are enforceable. Some companies move straight to statutory sick pay in these situations and the employee seeks part-time employment to subsidize their wages. Be sure you state your requirements as a company in these situations and ensure that the employment contract and employment laws are not conflicted.

Any activities of the employee that unduly delay the return or extend the need for treatment can invoke the company disciplinary procedure. Any cost volunteered by the company to the employee's treatment programme may be stopped. Before any such action is taken, ensure you have communicated and documented all situations directly with the employee.

Remember, if an employee self-refers a substance or alcohol misuse problem, it makes no difference whether you have a SAMP in place or not; they cannot be summarily dismissed under UK employment law. You as the employer are duty bound to help them go through a process, and that process is what you will be judged by.

Chapter summary

This chapter has made available a structured EAP approach that in my opinion is designed to provide a relevant employee with a dignified support mechanism. I have operated this approach now for over 20 years in one form or another. Many believed that they would be stigmatized by self-referral or the enrolment into an EAP, especially where there was no need for them to be suspended from work or have another work restriction applied. The truth of it is that the employee who is enrolled into the EAP has found that those colleagues who care rally around and become both supportive and protective.

Use this chapter to build a recovery-oriented EAP; be sure you consider all aspects of this chapter and above all use it to expand on and make it business /sector specific.

Do

1. Build your EAP before you announce the intention to start workplace substance and alcohol misuse testing, as you may get employee referrals immediately.
2. Structure the EAP so that there are enrolment, exclusion and removal criteria.
3. Once you have agreed on an EAP for an employee, make sure you set a recovery-oriented programme.
4. Rely on the reports of specialist intervention providers before you make any negative decision.
5. Examine the toxicology report to measure progress.
6. Always be ready to change the direction of the treatment.
7. Always be ready to review the employee's fitness for work, phased or full return.
8. Always consider the legal impact and breach of any insurance requirements.
9. Always consider how statutory requirements will impact your insurance coverage and culpabilities within civil and criminal legislations.
10. Examine T&Cs of employment around the EAP.
11. Consider reasonable adjustments around the EAP.
12. Make sure you have managed the time frame, removal criteria or opportunities to rehabilitate an employee enrolled in the EAP before you dismiss.

Do not

1. Ignore the need to respond to an employee self-referral.
2. Create unachievable goals within the EAP.

3. Ignore the respect the company will have from the whole workforce when they see the EAP being applied and proven to work regardless of what decision is made.
4. Think your efforts will go unrewarded or unnoticed.
5. Think you cannot dismiss an employee while they are on an enrolled programme
6. Ignore the need to publicize within the workplace and T&Cs of employment the fact that the company has an EAP programme with conditions.

5 | Alcohol and the workplace

Alcohol is a drug; it is classified as a depressant

- To celebrate events, achievements, etc., *some* people drink alcohol to excess. What is a depressant drug and why?
- When people are depressed some will see alcohol as a temporary relief but do not see it as a further depressant. Why?
- Like most depressant drugs, alcohol is not the answer to depression.
- The fact is, alcohol is a legal substance that when taken in moderation de-inhibits people and becomes the focus for socializing or a support mechanism to socializing.
- Alcohol can also be a gateway drug to other substance misuse issues.
- Alcohol dependency can be split into two scenarios, functioning dependency and non-functioning dependency.

Alcohol dependency has many other complications and attendant psychological/physical problems. For the purpose of the workplace, the employer has to be seen to manage the problem within the employee's Fiduciary Duty to be Fit for Work. This chapter is not the complete answer to general alcohol issues but provides information that is designed to help employers and employees make decisions about their individual responsibilities and potential support mechanisms. It should also aid the employer in creating strategies around how alcohol misuse by employees can negatively impact the business and the individual concerned. Problems occur, as with the misuse of any drug, at the point where people start to lose control of their user/drinking habits, whether temporarily or on a more long-term basis. Other issues revolve around the problems of a functioning alcohol abuser as opposed to a non-functioning alcohol abuser. Within the workplace the problems arise around the management of what is a legal substance being misused. Some people need to and do function under the influence of intoxicating liquor; others do not function at all in the same circumstances. The fact is both situations have to be managed as a risk to the individual and the company.

Alcohol Concern in the UK some time ago identified four levels of risk drinking and submitted numbers to indicate how many of each there were:

Lower risk drinkers. Men and women who regularly drink no more than 2 units of alcohol per day. Fourteen units per week are the maximum with advice to abstain on one or more consecutive days.

26 million lower risk drinkers in England.

Hazardous drinkers. Those who drink over sensible limits, either regularly or through less frequent sessions of heavy binge drinking. Hazardous drinkers have so far avoided alcohol-related harm. There is an increasing risk for men and women who regularly drink over the average of 2 units per day.

7.2 million increasing risk drinkers in England.

Harmful drinkers. Those usually drinking above sensible levels. Harmful drinkers can show evidence of some alcohol-related harm. Higher risk men who regularly drink over 8 units per day and women who regularly drink over 6 units per day. Higher risk individuals will have a higher alcohol tolerance, which may make them especially vulnerable to alcohol dependency.

1.4 million higher-risk drinkers in England.

Dependent drinkers. Those who are likely to have increased tolerance of alcohol, suffer withdrawal symptoms and have lost some degree of control over their drinking.

1.6 million dependent drinkers in England.

While it is clear the above statistics show that the vast majority of the UK drinking population is able to control its drinking habits there are still, however, a significant number of people who have issues that in time will have an on-cost to their own independent physical and mental wellbeing and a national on-cost into the UK's NHS. *What is the situation within your own country's alcohol demographics?* Alcohol misuse comes with a range of issues that have a negative impact on the individual and society, such as

Physical and social problems related to alcohol

- Cardiovascular disease
- Stroke/heart attack
- Cancer
- Malnutrition
- Gastrointestinal disorders
- Liver disease
- Dementia
- HIV/AIDS/sexual health issues
- Accidents (minor/serious/fatal)

Psychological issues related to alcohol

- Depression
- Apathy
- Isolation
- Loneliness
- Relationship problems
- Absenteeism from work which can lead to unemployment and a narrowing of social circles

General information for the UK (what is it in your country?)

- It is alleged that individuals in the UK are consuming more alcohol than they did 50 years ago.
- Consumption is rising in the UK, while allegedly falling in other countries with a similar population.
- People are drinking younger, longer, faster and more cheaply, across the class and gender spectrum.
- Over 1 million violent alcohol-related incidents occur.
- Thousands of incidents of domestic violence are linked to alcohol consumption.
- Increased anti-social behaviour and fear of crime are linked to alcohol consumption.

- Millions of pounds are spent on specialist alcohol treatment.
- In excess of 100,000 hospital admissions are alcohol related.
- Alcohol misuse accounts for around 40% of all UK admissions to Accident and Emergency (A&E) departments.
- Thousands of premature deaths per annum are alcohol related.
- Hundreds of suicides are alcohol related.
- Millions of lost working days are alcohol related.
- Over a million children are affected by parental alcohol problems, at least 200,000 of whose parents need a structured intervention/support.
- Increased divorce is linked to alcohol consumption.
- Deaths from liver cirrhosis have risen in Britain over 30 years by 959% for men aged 25–44 years and by 924% for women aged 25–44 years (Sir Richard Doll, 2004)
- 28% of high value branded alcohol in the UK is allegedly counterfeit.

Alcohol-related harm (estimated; most studies are 4–5 years behind actual information)

- £1.7 billion – NHS
- £95 million invested in specialist NHS alcohol treatment programmes
- £7+ billion – combat crime and anti-social behaviour
- £6+ billion incurred by loss of productivity
- £4+ billion human and emotional cost to family
  Total £21+ billion and rising

Income from alcoholic drinks (estimated)

- Income from drinks industry more than *£30 billion per year*
- Incorporating *£7 billion* in excise duties paid to the government
- 1 million jobs created, voracious advertising and sponsorship campaigns
- Industry income, *£30 billion* per year; alcohol-related harm, *£21+ billion per year*
  8 billion reasons why UK likely to continue with a culture of drinking-related harm and crime

Some alcohol-related treatment options

Depending on the nature of the individual and their journey through their drink-related issues there are a variety of ways to deal with alcohol misuse, many of which can be applied while in employment, but monitored for insurance risk and other legislation risk-related circumstances.

How alcohol misuse is treated depends on how much alcohol a person is consuming. The following are some of the types of intervention that could still be conducted while the person is in employment.

Some treatment options include

- **Detoxification** – involves a nurse or doctor supporting a person to safely stop drinking; this can be done by helping the person slowly cut down over a period of time or by providing medicines to prevent the experience of withdrawal.
- **Counselling** – including self-help groups and talking therapies such as cognitive behavioural therapy (CBT).
- **Medication** – there are two main types of medicines to help people stop drinking. The first is to help stop withdrawal symptoms and is given in decreasing doses over a short period of time. The most common medicine that is used in this way is chlordiazepoxide (Librium). The second is medications to reduce any urge to have a drink. The most common medications used for this purpose are acamprosate and naltrexone, which are given at a fixed dose for 6–12 months. As time goes by other drugs will be made available to assist alcohol consumption issues.

Extended brief intervention

Extended brief intervention (EBI) is a one-to-one session with a healthcare professional, usually a doctor, nurse or counsellor. It takes the form of a motivational interviewing technique. The aim is to motivate people to change their behaviour by exploring with them why they drink in the way they do and help them identify positive reasons for changing.

FRAMES is an acronym that's often used to describe the components of a brief intervention. It stands for

- **F**eedback – on your risk of having alcohol problems
- **R**esponsibility – helping you take responsibility for change
- **A**dvice – providing clear advice when requested
- **M**enu – explaining the options for change
- **E**mpathy – an approach that's warm, reflective and understanding
- **S**elf – Efficacy – helping you believe in your ability to change

Cognitive behavioural therapy

Cognitive behavioural therapy (CBT) is a talking therapy that uses a problem-solving approach to alcohol dependence. CBT's approach to alcohol dependence is to identify unhelpful and unrealistic thoughts and beliefs that may be contributing to alcohol dependence, such as:

- 'I can't relax without alcohol.'
- 'My friends would find me boring if I was sober.'
- 'Just drinking one pint can't hurt.'

Once such thoughts and beliefs are identified, the individual would be encouraged to base their behaviour on more realistic and helpful thoughts such as:

- 'Lots of people have good times without alcohol and I can be one of them.'
- 'My friends like me for my personality, not for my drinking.'
- 'I know I can't stop drinking once I start.'

CBT also helps identify triggers that can cause a person to drink, such as:

- Stress
- Social anxiety
- Being in 'high risk' environments such as pubs, clubs and restaurants

A CBT therapist will *try* to teach an individual how to avoid certain triggers and how to cope effectively with those that are unavoidable.

It is clear that chronic alcohol misuse requires a higher degree of intervention that may preclude the employee from attending work or rendering them as unemployable for a period of time. As an employer/employee it is worth repeating that *it is an employee's Fiduciary Duty to be Fit for Work* and it is on that basis that the employer must manage an alcohol-related workplace situation.

Workplace alcohol countermeasures

There are a number of countermeasures for managing alcohol misuse issues in the workplace. They can include, in no particular order:

- Terms and conditions (T&Cs) of the employee's contract
- Enhanced induction training and recording protocols
- Substance and alcohol misuse policy application
- Education within the workplace
- Poster campaigns within the workplace
- Breath alcohol testing
- Application of the company Employee Assistance Programme (EAP)
- Testing for alcohol using toxicology via urine or hair analysis
- Other policies around driving a company vehicle

Remember: A breath-alcohol (BA) test device, whether Home Office type approved or not, is just a screening device, *it is not an evidential device in the UK*. To dismiss an employee purely on the result of a screening breath test device, in my opinion, is not legal in UK employment law. The deep lung breath-alcohol *screening device* is used to detect a legal substance above an agreed on cut-off that if breached can invoke the disciplinary procedure or be subject to the Road Traffic Act. It's at this point we have to stop and think that the invoking of disciplinary procedures up to and including dismissal also applies to the use of illegal substances, illegal activity or failing to comply with statutory requirements.

Examples

1. An employee comes to work below the UK legal drink-drive limit of 35 micrograms (mcg) per 100 millilitres (ml) of breath but above the company cut-off, which is set at 15 mcg. *What do you do?*

Your decision revolves around the fact that the employee can legally drive a vehicle on a public road. They have breached the company policy for the alcohol limit. Do you dismiss them under these circumstances? Your approach would be significantly more severe than that of a magistrate's court if they were over the legal limit under the UK Road Traffic Act.

2. An employee who has an alcohol problem is found drinking during working hours. They are functioning but are above the company cut-off and legal drink drive cut-off. The employee does not hold a driving licence but does drive other vehicles (forklifts, etc.) during work or away from work. *What do you do?*

   Your decision revolves around the fact you have a policy limit. The Road Traffic Act is irrelevant to the company in this situation. Is the incident a one-off or has it repeated over the years? Alcohol dependency is an illness, just like any other illness. Can we use the EAP for the start of evaluation and management of repeat offending?

3. An employee declares their substance and alcohol misuse to the UK Driver and Vehicle Licensing Agency (DVLA), as a statutory requirement. DVLA takes their licence from them while they are receiving confidential treatment for a limited period of time in assessment of their continued fitness to hold a driving licence. They have a driving position at work, both on and away from site. They have not told you the employer they have had their licence suspended while they are in treatment and an incident has occurred in the workplace involving them using a forklift. You have or do not have T&Cs around such declarations. *What do you do in either situation? What have you done to prevent these situations?*

   Your decision revolves around whether or not they are now fit for purpose under their T&Cs of employment. How long will they require treatment? Are there any reasonable adjustments available? What happens if DVLA keep them from getting their licence back?

4. An employee has lost their driving licence at the magistrates' court, having been prosecuted by the police for a drink driving offence. They have not told their employer and continue driving a company vehicle. *What do you do? What have you put in place to manage this eventuality?*

   Your decision revolves around what T&Cs you have in place. Have you had employees sign and agree to tell you of their loss of licence or imminent loss due to build-up of points, etc.? Has this issue been identified as a gross misconduct in T&Cs?

5. An employee is found to be above the legal drink drive limit at work and is suspended until they are fit to be interviewed. They insist they are going to drive their car home. The car is parked on company property. *What do you do?*
    *   *Can you stop them driving their own car off site? No.*
    *   *Can you take their car keys away from them? No.*
    *   *Can you detain them until the police arrive? No.*
    *   *It's the end of their shift pattern. Can you detain them beyond the end of the shift? No.*

Your decisions revolve around the answers to the four questions and your powers of detention/removal of private property from the owner.

Each of the above situations is an event that has happened in the workplace. These and others will continue to happen. There is a need to manage two types of situation::

1. Where an employee is required to drive on or away from a public road in a company vehicle.
2. Where employees who do not drive on site or on a public road but have duties within the company that may or may not be risk positions.

With each of the two points above there is a need to ensure that you as the employer have created the right environment to challenge each situation as it comes to notice, and you can manage the situation legally. To do that, there is a need to first of all ensure that:

*   T&Cs of employment are correct.
*   Enhanced induction and training records are comprehensive.
*   You have created an EAP where these situations or appropriate scenarios, such as self-referral, are confidentially managed before any affirmative action is taken.
*   You have a means to test an individual and manage the result.
*   Most importantly, your SAMP is legally enforceable.

Some of the situations are continuous offences against UK law and a disciplinary application is obvious. The five areas and the other areas outlined in the workplace testing countermeasures paragraph are the firm basis by which you should build your case for the correct and measured outcome of an alcohol misuse situation in the workplace. When dealing with either illegal or legal substance misuse there is a need to apply the judgement process on a consistent basis that can be defended if or when challenged.

A specialist provider should have a number of packages available that are designed specifically for workplace solutions. The responsibility for making them effective in the workplace for an employee is with the employer and the management team supported by a qualified service provider.

Testing methodologies for alcohol

There are a number of ways to test for alcohol in the body. As with substance misuse testing, those methods can detect recent use as well as historical/cumulative misuse.

The workplace has a need to examine an employee's fitness for work within a variety of circumstances around alcohol, which can include:

- For cause/post-incident
- Routine, human asset management
- Rehabilitation
- Unusual demeanour
- Smell of intoxicating liquor
- Role or sector-specific, device attached to vehicle ignition, pre-flight, etc.
- On entering or leaving bonded warehouse operations and so on

When choosing an alcohol breath test device there is a need to consider the current standards of the employee T&Cs, the strength of the SAMP and POT and so on, before you move to the following guidance.

Question

Is an employee less able for work if they exhale 34 or 36 mcg per 100 ml of breath? The only difference is that one is legal for driving a vehicle on a road and the other is not and comes with a power of arrest for a constable in uniform if the employee is driving on a public road.

Question

Is someone who is at twice the legal drink drive limit fit for work or not, if they are functioning normally?

The fact is a breath test device and the Road Traffic Act set a standard for driving a motor vehicle on a road. Alcohol can be measured using a single type of test device, whereas a drug cannot. Alcohol is legal where illicit drugs are not. Be sure you have your policy and support mechanisms correct before you examine the severity of the action you take.

Alcohol breath test (observed narrow-window collection)

A variety of breath test devices are available for use. The UK police are required to use Home Office (HO) type approved equipment for the purposes of enforcement across the variety of road traffic acts. HO type approval empowers a *constable in uniform* to arrest and detain a positive donor for further analysis on different *'evidential'* equipment while in custody or via a blood or urine submission for confirmation at an approved laboratory.

In the workplace (commerce and industry) there is no power of arrest and detention. Just as the POC screening devices for illegal drugs are non-evidential, so it is for the workplace breath test device. The breath test device is a screening device for a legal substance. Why would it become an evidential device because you have a SAMP in place? Companies and managers need to think very hard on any action they take with regard to a breath test device. Some of the aforementioned circumstances highlight the complicated nature of screening a legal substance.

At Hall & Angus we have access to different types of devices. Our recommended workplace unit is the Alco-Sensor FST, which has multiple capabilities that include:

- The obvious deep lung breath test capability.
- A passive cup application for rapid mass screening.
- A detector for examining liquids for alcohol content.
- Very robust for workplace use and comes with or without a printer.

The EAP is a consideration to be applied for alcohol misuse, where employers have such a provision to employees. As with substance misuse, people can default into alcohol misuse for a great many reasons.

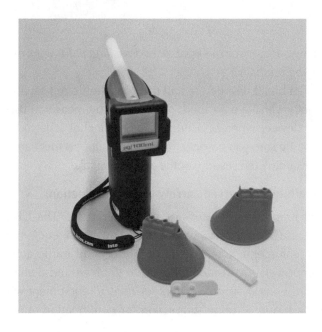

Figure 5.1 Intoximeter Breath test device (courtesy of Intoximeter).

Alcohol can also be measured in hair. Situations have occurred in which a hair analysis is used in rehabilitation to measure progress or to identify how chronic the alcohol misuse/dependency is.

The drink and drive legislations in this book highlight some of the UK penalties. In the workplace, the outcome can be much more catastrophic for those who fall foul of the situation. In law, on conviction of a drink driving offence you would likely:

- Lose your licence for at least one year.
- Receive a fine of no less than £1,000, or if you are a high earner you may receive a fine that is means tested against your annual income and considered against first or repeat offences.
- Have points added to your licence.
- Incur higher insurance costs.

An employee may or may not lose their job as a result of a positive breath test under the Road Traffic Act. In the workplace, depending on policy construction, T&Cs of employment and other countermeasures applied by the company this is the very thing you are looking at as a consequence of a positive breath test. In the event you are considering dismissal of an employee based on the results of a non-evidential device, the employee:

- Will keep their driving licence where there is no police action.
- May or may not lose their job, depending on the employer's approach to the matter.
- Will experience a financial impact, to themselves and their family, that will be far more than that imposed by any court in terms of loss of annual salary, lifestyle, etc.
- Faces potential isolation within their community.

I would urge employers to seriously consider whether or not their policy is robust enough with regard to alcohol testing, if they even have a policy. If they do not have a robust policy, then the problems escalate and counter-measures that can be applied are restricted.

If you are an employee who has been dismissed as a result of a positive test on a non-evidential device, you certainly should consider seeking legal advice on the basis that the dismissal was potentially unlawful and dependent on an examination of the content of the company SAMP, POT and T&Cs of employment.

So, let's clear up the UK situation with regard to the use of breath test devices in the workplace.

Types of breath test devices

- Home Office (HO) type approved with digital read screen and calibration certificate (with or without printer)
- Non-HO type approved with digital read screen calibration certificate (with or without printer)
- Use for installation into vehicles via the ignition system and a tethered breath test device
- Wall mounted for installation into warehouse operations, tachograph issue, key cabinets, vehicle telematics, etc.
- Reusable devices with digital screen for personal use or provision to staff
- HO type approved disposable devices (blow in the bag)

I cannot repeat enough: the most important consideration with regard to alcohol breath test devices is that they are *non-evidential screening devices* (at the time of going to print).

The HO type approved devices have gone through an accreditation process and have met standards for:

- Accuracy deviations/parameters
- Interference substances
- Temperature fluctuations
- Robustness/durability
- Repeatability of sample analysis
- Use in high wind and more

It's because of these accreditations/qualifications we recommend a UK HO breath test unit to give the workplace programme a level of application above other types of breath test units which have questionable results or standards of operation.

If a positive sample is provided by the driver of a vehicle on a public road above any of the UK drink/drug driving limits the driver will be arrested and detained under the Road Traffic Act. The driver is taken back to a police station, where they remain under arrest and taken through a process using an evidential breath device, significantly different from a roadside screening device. The donor can also choose blood or urine back to laboratory analysis as another option. If the arrested person refuses to be tested on any of those options after arrest they are prosecuted under the act for refusing a lawful request. On conviction they will likely lose their driving licence and be fined, all of which are enforced by law within the Criminal Justice System (CJS).

So, what is the approach from the employer who wants to use breath test devices to protect the individual, the directors and the company from prosecution where criminal and civil legislations can be and are applied to a wide variety of workplace alcohol-related situations? What are the circumstances that workplace breath testing can be applied to and what are the limits that can be set?

Workplace applications of breath alcohol testing

A quick quiz:

1. *What is the alcohol limit that can be set by a company?*
2. *Does it have to be the maximum drink drive limit for the country in which the company or its employees are operating in?*

3. *Are the alcohol limits of other companies applicable to you or your employees while working or visiting their operations?*
4. *Are there sector-specific legal limits?*
5. *Are there job-specific legal limits which are mandated?*

Some UK drug driving penalties

You could be imprisoned, banned from driving and face a fine if you're found guilty of drink and/or drug driving. The actual penalty you get is up to the magistrates who hear your individual case, and depends on your specific circumstances, offence and annual income.

You may be able to reduce your ban by taking a drink-drive rehabilitation scheme (DDRS) course if you're banned from driving for 12 months or more. It's up to the court to offer this.

Refusing to provide a specimen of breath, blood or urine for analysis

You may receive:

- 6 months' imprisonment
- Up to £5,000 fine
- A ban from driving for at least 1 year

Causing death by careless driving when under the influence of drink/drugs

You may receive:

- 14 years' imprisonment
- An unlimited fine
- A ban from driving for at least 2 years
- An extended driving test before your licence is returned

The high-risk offenders scheme

Your driving licence won't be returned automatically at the end of a driving ban if you're a 'high-risk offender'. You'll get your licence back only if you pass a medical examination.

You're a high-risk offender if you

- Were convicted of 2 drink-driving offences within 10 years.
- Were driving with an alcohol reading of at least 87.5 micrograms of alcohol per 100 millilitres of breath, 200 milligrams of alcohol per 100 millilitres of blood, or 267.5 milligrams of alcohol per 100 millilitres of urine.
- Refused to give the police a sample of breath, blood or urine to test for alcohol.
- Refused to allow a sample of your blood to be tested for alcohol (e.g., if it was taken when you were unconscious).

Other problems you could face

A conviction for drink/drug driving also means:

- Your car insurance costs will increase significantly.
- If you drive for work, your employer will see your conviction on your licence.
- You may have trouble travelling to countries like the USA.

Which drugs does the ban include?

Illegal substances such as ketamine, LSD, cocaine, cannabis and heroin will be screened in 'zero-tolerance' legislation through the use of roadside 'drugalysers' – that work similar to breathalysers – and also urine/blood tests at police stations.

Table of drugs and limits

'Illegal' drugs ('accidental exposure' – zero tolerance approach)	Threshold limit in blood
Benzoylecgonine	50 µg/L
Cocaine	10 µg/L
Delta-9-tetrahydrocannabinol (cannabis)	2 µg/L
Ketamine	20 µg/L
Lysergic acid diethylamide	1 µg/L
Methylamphetamine	10 µg/L
MDMA	10 µg/L
6-Monoacetylmorphine (heroin)	5 µg/L

'Medicinal' drugs (risk-based approach)	Threshold limit in blood
Amphetamine	250 μg/L
Clonazepam	50 μg/L
Diazepam	550 μg/L
Flunitrazepam	300 μg/L
Lorazepam	100 μg/L
Methadone	500 μg/L
Morphine	80 μg/L
Oxazepam	300 μg/L
Temazepam	1,000 μg/L

There are strict alcohol limits for drivers, but it's impossible to say exactly how many drinks this equals, as the metabolization of alcohol is different for each person depending on a variety of situations around food consumption and other scenarios.

The drink driving limits in the UK are currently (at the time of going to press)

Level of alcohol	England, Wales, Northern Ireland	Scotland
Micrograms per 100 millilitres of breath	35	22
Milligrams per 100 millilitres of blood	80	50
Milligrams per 100 millilitres of urine	107	67

Employer's workplace initiatives towards alcohol, substance misuse/dependencies

- Control of alcohol in the workplace, lunchtime drinking, salesforce/ employee/ contractor activity off or away from site.
- Alcohol testing and policy enforcement, use of machinery/vehicles, on– off site etc.
- Substance misuse testing and enforcement with specific reference to the UK drug driving regulations.
- Employment T&Cs and policy endorsements.
- Confidential self-referral procedures, cannot dismiss.
- Employee Assistance Programme (EAP).

- Rehabilitation support and clinical interventions, costs and structure.
- Proactive in-house advertising re alcohol and substance abuse and its ramifications.
- Whistle-blowing programme 24/7.
- Awareness training to personnel records.
- Leadership training to personnel records.
- Data Protection Act.
- Purchase of test equipment.
- Union and Works Counsel activity.
- Health & safety activity.
- HR activity.
- Poster campaigns.
- Helplines/whistleblowing facility.

Employee responsibilities

- To comply with the drink and drug driving laws en route to, during or outside of work.
- To comply with statutes regarding use, possession, distribution and production of illicit substances under a variety of acts.
- To comply with the Medicines Act with regard to prescribed medicines.
- To comply with the employer's policies and procedures.
- To comply with the T&Cs of employment.
- To meet a fiduciary duty to be fit for work.

You cannot dismiss an employee based on the result of a drug screening device, those that are instant POC devices for illegal/legal substance misuse.

What makes it any more legal to dismiss an employee based on the results of an alcohol screening device that measures the level of a legal substance? The fact is, the cut-off for alcohol is either applied under the Road Traffic Act or is a mandatory level set for specific sectors and job descriptions.

Example

For pilots/air crew and air traffic controllers, the maximum detectable alcohol limit is 9 micrograms of alcohol per 100 millilitres of breath. For all other staff, such as fuel tanker drivers, those who tow aircraft full of passengers and so on, in England and Wales, the limit is the legal drink-drive limit of 35 micrograms of alcohol in every 100 millilitres of breath. Other professions have similar restrictions.

Chapter summary

The whole subject area of alcohol in the workplace is more complicated than companies and managers think. There are variables that do not exist with the detection of illegal substances. Few people have given thought to the fact a breath alcohol device in the UK is a *non-evidential device*, it makes no difference whether it is calibrated or not. Calibration merely shows a device was measured and tested on a given day and was at the time accurate. The use of a breath alcohol device is the start of a process that relies very much on T&Cs of employment and the strength of the SAMP to proceed towards summary dismissal. Consideration needs to be given as to how you manage a positive breath test and the circumstances that surround it. You may find that in the future, more employees will challenge a dismissal for a positive breath test that is applicable to the Road Traffic Act but applied to a non-related workplace situation.

At Hall and Angus we have a range of legally defensible responses to a variety of alcohol-related situations, in many, dismissal is the second choice. The EAP is the answer to most.

Do

1. Make sure you set an alcohol cut-off within your SAMP that is no higher than the legal limit to drive. You can set any limit you like.
2. Make sure your response to a negative situation is appropriate and consistent with the company's approach on such matters.
3. Provide poster campaigns around the workplace with regard to the relevant laws and the company's approach on such matters.
4. Make sure you have appropriate alcohol test equipment available in the workplace.
5. Make sure you have staff who are trained in how to use your chosen test equipment.
6. Make sure the test equipment is calibrated within the manufacturer's guidelines.
7. Make sure your T&Cs of employment are sufficient for your company needs with regard to alcohol and those who drive on the company's behalf.
8. Comply with your legal duty to report drink driving offences/offenders to the police.

Do not

1. Ignore your responsibilities around workplace alcohol misuse.
2. Ignore seasonal or event-specific drink-drive campaigns operated by UK police forces or your own country campaigns.
3. Leave the onus on the employee to tell you they have lost their license. It needs to be a T&C of employment that they comply with your identified and signed T&Cs.
4. Take a person's car keys from them. It is their private property.
5. Do not detain employees who seek to drive their own vehicle on a road against your advice. You must contact the police as soon as possible you know they will drive their car on a public road.
6. Fail to conduct poster campaigns or shift briefings around alcohol-related issues in the workplace.

6 | Workplace culture mapping (Formula-9-Plus)

Introduction

At Hall & Angus we have developed a confidential *'Electronic Workplace Culture Map'* (EWCM) that embraces a variety of weighted and stress-tested questions that help identify a wide range of workplace issues that may be occurring on site or influenced by on-site activity or by activities of employees off site. Some of these situations are identified in the mental and physical wellbeing of an employee and remain undetected and mismanaged by the company without the two-way street of engagement between employer and employee.

Using the culture mapping results, we are able to analyse and manage the negatives out of the workplace while at the same time identifying and enhancing the positives. Used on an annual basis, the EWCM also helps identify appropriate budget allocations and review the existing state of affairs around the positives and negatives of the programme while exposing the need for more innovative solutions to ongoing needs, whether your company is young or well established.

The culture map is confidential in the source of its information and is also designed to identify and manage risk within the business. The culture mapping exercise is extremely useful to assess where your workplace culture is before the start of a Programme Of Testing (POT). Not only will the culture map help the POT but it can also be applied at any time, year by year, to measure the effects of managing risk and the justification and quantification of given projects, subsequent budget allocations and much more.

On completion of the online initiative (2 weeks), Hall & Angus will then analyse and present the overall report; see the text that follows for sample questions and assessment charts. Hall & Angus will then work with the client to provide workplace enhancement initiatives and innovative management practices that provide a significant workplace return on investment (WROI) which allows companies to examine where they were, where they are and where they are going with regard to:

- Budget allocations and identification of the correct size of budget.
- Employee engagement and monitoring thereof, breaking down attitudes at varying durations of employment. *Are new employees better motivated than those who 10+ years of service?*
- Company reputation and stability.
- Pre-employment strategies.
- Management training.
- Staff training and awareness.
- Inward investment strategies.
- Attitudes of the employees to initiatives/management strategies.
- Compliance with and commitment to health & safety.
- Market position development, and so on.

Collectively, these approaches are restricted only by the imagination of what you want to get from the existing or a bespoke design EWCM, which can include sector- or other company-specific questions. The standard package EWCM was designed to examine and identify the following:

1. Employee mental health and physical wellbeing issues/solutions.
2. Health & safety issues and solutions.
3. The impact of smoking in the workplace and smoking cessation activities.
4. The impact of prescribed medications in the workplace (current Hall & Angus study).
5. Alcohol User Disorder Information Test (AUDIT).
6. Drug User Disorder Information Test (DUDIT).
7. Workplace criminality: what is really going on.
8. Whistle-blowing: who, what, when, where, why.

9. A 350-character free text box at the end of each section for the employee to say what they want about each section or other issues that concern them. Hence the EWCM now being called Formula-9-Plus

By using this approach on behalf of our clients we are able to consider the varieties of workplace cultures/attitudes with regard to company initiatives, the employees' ability to self-assess and manage their own situations, management strategies, budget allocations, and quantifying project effectiveness. The EWCM also has the ability to report year-by-year progress with the additional benefit of the employer engaging with its workforce with their consent and proactive input.

The Drug User Disorder Identifications Test (DUDIT) and the Alcohol Use Disorder Identifications Test (AUDIT) are formulas used in assessing the current state of an individual who is misusing or has a dependency on substances or alcohol. Another approach is the analysis of people's Perceptions, Opinions or Beliefs (POB). Hall and Angus have combined these approaches and modified them to discover the actual positives and negatives within a company's approach to the management of workplace initiatives that in the past may have required a significant and unnecessary budget allocation. We identify with, use and have modified those formulas alongside others and enhanced the menu of initiatives, each designed to provide proactive and appropriate reactive countermeasures, supported by our own professional intervention and rapid response teams.

POBs are also covered in Chapter 2 for the purpose of that application. With regard to the culture mapping, the POBs are expanded across a range of applications specifically to benefit the workplace, the employee and the management of risk.

Perceptions

(a) Some people's perceptions, which vary across generations and individual experiences, is that drug use is one big laugh and not that dangerous, or if it is dangerous, it's dangerous for someone else.
(b) Some managers have a perception that they are good managers and have had enough training and experience for the position they are in.

(c) We do not have a health & safety problem in our workplace.

(d) Drug testing is an expensive on-cost to the business.

(e) Drug and alcohol testing will disrupt my business and I will find it harder to recruit.

Opinions

(a) Some people's opinion is that alcoholics or those with drug dependencies have brought those problems upon themselves and that criminality plays a large part in their lives.

(b) Drugs should be legalized.

(c) What I do on my own time is my affair.

(d) What an employee does in their own time is their affair; we just want them fit for work.

(e) Health & safety is a waste of time when they keep giving me defective equipment and my colleagues are still under the influence of drugs and alcohol at work anyway.

Beliefs

(a) Some people believe that everyone who takes drugs is infected with a wide variety of contagious diseases or are on long-term treatment programmes.

(b) Some people believe that drug testing is against their human rights.

(c) Some people believe you can legally grow three cannabis plants for your own use.

(d) Some people believe they will lose half of their workforce if they start drug and alcohol testing.

(e) Some believe the company is doing the wrong things in the wrong way and consulting those who know how to do it better and cheaper is not being done.

There are many more POBs that company owners, managers and employees can bring to the table. The main questions are:

- *How have you identified them?*
- *How have you qualified them?*
- *If they are true what are you planning to do about it?*

- *Having decided on a course of action, how do you measure it against expectations?*

Confidential electronic workplace culture mapping is important at the start of any project of employee engagement being considered by our client and its management team. At the point of major change-management, the EWCM is the first thing to consider. The implementation team/steering committee needs to identify cost-effective, easy transition solutions that are progressive and proactive in the examination of:

1. Its own perceptions, opinions or beliefs, which also need to be stress tested and eliminated, modified or adopted.
2. The identification of the correct workplace incentives, which is the driving factor of employee engagement from the start.
3. The Identification of the most appropriate budget. Finance departments will certainly have an easier transition into identifying those that have a chance of success as well as those that are non-cost-effective initiatives/projects.
4. The identification of issues that as yet may have gone unnoticed or are not considered important to the employer but certainly important to the employee.
5. Who is best positioned within the company to conduct cost-effective initiatives or who is the best external supplier for those initiatives and who is best positioned to manage and report on them?
6. The identification of effective managers as well as those who require additional training or removal from their positions. You can have the best initiative available, but if the management team does not have the ability or belief to deliver it, then it will likely fail.
7. Examining different departmental issues/failings. Total buy-in across all departments and the impact to those departments post-ECWM is essential. It becomes very clear who is non-compliant or is a square peg in a round hole.
8. Above all, the ability to establish *FACT* and move forward from a firm and considered baseline:
    - Fact will identify the negatives and help manage them out of the business.
    - Fact will identify the positives and provide enhancement to what works.

- Fact will identify what is missing from the business within the structure of the EWCM.
- Fact will identify what can be brought to the business for the benefit of all.

The following is a selection of sample questions and responses that were fed back by the employees to an existing anonymous client. Many of the responses were not what was expected and shocked senior managers, directors and business owners. The following observations are a real-time snapshot of the business from the ground up and the management structure down. While the questions rely on the honesty and integrity of the employee, regardless of position, there is nothing to benefit anyone who lies where the answers are used to make the workplace a better place to be year by year. For that reason, deliberate misinformation is easy to identify and eliminate.

The workplace culture map can be designed and used to assess:

- Single-site operations
- Multisite operations
- Shift patterns
- Across all departments
- Within single departments
- Sector-specific situations

The following are true responses to four questions from each section within a client EWCM survey. Each section varies from 7 to 20 questions plus a 350-character free text box at the end of each section for employees to whistle-blow anonymously, clear the air on any topic not covered or where they feel there is a point to be made that concerns or impacts their colleagues, which they can address in their own words. Some questions are a simple Yes/No answer and others are graded 1–4, with 4 being the highest risk. The overall report is summarized on a Red, Amber, Green (RAG) report, with green being low risk, amber medium and red high. The percentage response/ scoring highlighted some of the issues that the client did not expect and thought were all under control or were not a problem.

Mental and physical wellbeing questions (20 questions): Overall assessment chart

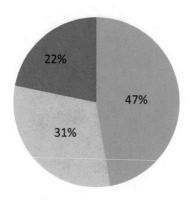

Sample questions

Q. How often is your physical or mental wellbeing affected by the time you get to work?
A. **Low = 36%; Medium = 73%; High = 27%**

Q. How often is the workplace the cause of your impaired physical or mental wellbeing?
A. **Low = 18%; Medium = 73%; High = 9%**

Q. Do you feel work negatively impacts your health?
A. **Low = 18%; Medium = 55%; High = 27%**

Q. Do you feel positive about your workplace prospects?
A. **Low = 55%; Medium = 0%; High = 45%** (This was a Yes/No question.)

Smoking questions (7 questions, smoker only response): Overall assessment chart

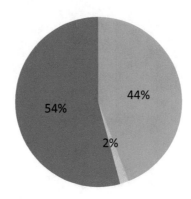

Sample questions

Q. Does smoking at work help you control your dependency or workplace stress level?

A. **Low = 0%; Medium = 0%; High = 100%**

Q. Are you currently using or has your employer provided any nicotine replacement therapies?

A. **Low = 14%; Medium = 0%; High = 86%** (This was a Yes/No question.)

Q. Is black market tobacco available in your workplace?

A. **Low = 71%; Medium = 0%; High = 29%** (This was a Yes/No question.)

Q. Does your employer provide a programme to help you stop smoking?

A. **Low = 29%; Medium = 0%; High = 71%** (This was a Yes/No question.)

Health & safety questions (11 questions, all Yes/ No answers): Overall assessment chart

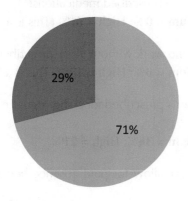

Sample questions

Q. Does your workplace conduct regular health & safety briefings?
A. **Low = 55%; Medium = 0%; High = 45%**

Q. Have you ever had to work without or with defective personal protective equipment?
A. **Low = 73%; Medium = 0%; High = 27%**

Q. Have you ever been a victim of someone else's lack of health & safety compliance?
A. **Low = 64%; Medium = 0%; High = 36%**

Q. Have you ever reported a health & safety issue at work?
A. **Low = 55%; Medium = 0%; High = 45%**

Prescribed medication questions (10 questions)

> *Note: Assessment Chart withheld for completion of 2-year workplace study around prescribed medication impact in the workplace.*

Sample questions

Q. Do you currently take prescribed medications?
A. **Low = 39%; Medium = 0%; High = 61%** (This is a Yes/No question.)

Q. Could you still attend work without those prescribed medications?
A. **Low = 82%; Medium = 0%; High = 18%** (This is a Yes/No question.)

Q. Are your medications prescribed for a short-term, medium-term or long-term condition?
A. **Low = 33%; Medium = 36%; High = 21%**

Q. Does your employer allow for paid absence because of your medical condition?
A. **Low = 0%; Medium = 0%; High = 100%** (This is a Yes/No question.)

***AUDIT, Alcohol User Disorder Information Test
(16 questions): Overall assessment chart***

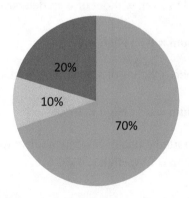

Sample questions

Q. How often have you had 6 or more units of alcohol on a single occasion in the last 12 months?
A. **Low = 11%; Medium = 56%; High = 33%**

Q. How often in the past 12 months have you not been in a state of good health to perform your work duties due to alcohol?
A. **Low = 67%; Medium = 22%; High = 11%**

Q. How often during the last 12 months have you not attended work due to alcohol?
A. **Low = 100%; Medium 0%; High = 0%**

Q. Does your employer provide you with a confidential route to self-refer an alcohol issue?
A. **Low = 27%; Medium = 0%; High = 73%** (This was a Yes/No question.)

DUDIT, Drug User Disorder Information Test Questions
(15 questions): Overall assessment chart

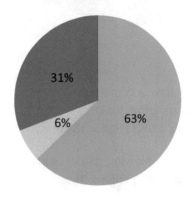

Sample questions

Q. Have you ever used illegal substances for recreational purposes?
A. **Low = 64%; Medium = 0%; High = 36%** (This is a Yes/No question.)

Q. How often during the last 12 months have you had a feeling of guilt or remorse because of your use of illegal drugs?
A. **Low = 33%; Medium = 33%; High = 34%**

Q. Have you ever been in treatment for dependency issues around illegal substances?
A. **Low = 82%; Medium = 0%; High = 18%** (This is a Yes/No question.)

Workplace criminality and whistle-blowing (10 questions, mostly Yes/No)

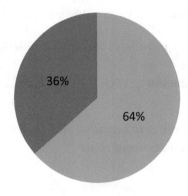

Sample questions

Q. Does your company have a confidential means to whistle-blow on workplace criminality or any other topic?
A. **Low = 82%; Medium = 0%; High = 18%**

Q. Do you trust the whistle-blowing system employed by your company?
A. **Low = 64%; Medium = 0%; High = 36%**

Q. If you were aware of or witnessed criminal activity in the workplace would you report it using the whistle-blowing protocol?
A. **Low = 73%; Medium = 0%; High = 27%**

Q. Is criminal activity occurring in your workplace?
A. **Low = 73%; Medium = 0%; High = 27%**

The assessment charts and questions are an easy indicator of which areas to attack for immediate action and another strategy around medium- to long-term issues. The assessment charts when compared across multisite operations quickly identify glaring differences between sites, allowing for the additional assessment of best practice under different management styles/priorities. The following are some other observations where the employer/employee can both help benefit from the workplace EWCM as a whole with observations around:

1. There is non-compliance by the workforce.
2. There is non-compliance/enforcement by the management team/employer.

Workplace culture mapping (Formula-9-Plus)

3. Despite some employees not being fit for work they still attended.
4. Some results did not reveal the full truth of the situation on closer examination and the exposure was worse than admitted when dealt with.
5. Failure on the side of the business and the management of existing protocols.
6. Failure with regard to policy enforcement/compliance of existing protocols.
7. Employees of all levels had a say in the delivery of identifiable issues in which they, so far, had no input capability.
8. Employees of all levels had the opportunity to put forward solutions via the free text box where they had previously not been consulted.
9. Employees of all levels were able to provide/suggest new initiatives that were beneficial to all and were specific to a controlled set of questions.
10. The EWCM also catered for additional questions to be asked on the next survey as a result of the general circulation of results.

So, why is the EWCM important within the context of this book and its guide to managing workplace substance misuse? The truth of the matter is it all revolves around the mental and physical wellbeing of the workforce and those who are charged to manage it.

Mental and physical wellbeing in the workplace can be impacted in a vast array of situations that already exist in the individual, the employment pool, the local community or existing workplace culture. Substance and alcohol misuse brings with it a range of negatives that can be exacerbated by all other question areas of the survey and each chapter in this book. There is a need to identify what the overall problem is and how the business approaches and manages the subject. There is also a need to drill down into an individual's needs, as outlined in Chapter 4 on the EAP. There is a need to manage an individual with consistency and fairness as outlined in Chapter 3 on the Substance and Alcohol Abuse Policy (SAMP). A company will invest a significant sum of money in an individual who is expected to be productive and happy in their work:

- *How do we measure that?*
- *How do you deliver that?*
- *Where do you set a level that is the measure of acceptability in the workplace?*
- *How can you exceed that measure and continue to raise the bar?*

This book and the EWCM are designed to help that process.

Health & safety in the workplace sets a different set of parameters, many of which are legislated for and many of which have serious consequences when not applied or are disregarded by an employee who needs to be trained and guided. Health & safety in the workplace started with the need to have a competent person delivering common-sense approaches to protect the business and those who work within it. It has now moved on to be the cornerstone of all things safety with an overarching regulatory executive, prosecution status around failure and a growing demand for qualifications for those who practise the trade. A SAMP, POT and EAP are introduced under health & safety. You can have as many training programmes as you like, you can have as many policies and protocols as you like, but the first and foremost protocol must be: *'Is the employee complying with their Fiduciary Duty to be Fit for Work?'* Fit for work includes the ability to comply with health & safety policies and protocols, all applied to the governance of the business. The same is true of HR, occupational health, procurement, and off course of any legal framework. All professions have a part to play in the development and management of a complete workplace substance and alcohol misuse programme, though few have the ability to build or guide the process in its entirety. None are trained in the wider design and development; none have a point of reference to draw down on. The analytical laboratory industry is no better, as they operate within the constraints of accreditations and the need for the chain of custody to be complete on submission to the laboratory. This is generally where their support ends.

This book and the EWCM help with that process.

Prescribed medications in the workplace have both negative and positive impacts. The negatives are that some people are not fit for work due to the side effects of their medications but still attend. Some of those medications have short-, medium- and long-term prescribing windows that require the EAP approach or a reasonable adjustment to facilitate employment under controlled circumstances outside of a risk assessment of the employee's role. Some medications are subject specifically to the UK drug driving regulations, and the regulations apply to all medications where the medication is causing the driver to be impaired and therefore not fit to drive a vehicle. Many medications are prescribed by GPs beyond the manufacturer's guidelines and lead to other user disorders and the building of a patient's tolerance to the drug, which then requires titration and subsequent dependency treatment.

The positives are the fact that many people attend work because they are taking prescribed medications that help them manage symptoms that would otherwise be debilitating. The managing of prescribed medications has to be considered in the workplace, the policy and role/job-specific terms and conditions situations where risk is being applied. In the UK part B of the prescription is the proof that an employee is legally entitled to possess and use those drugs as prescribed, many of which are controlled substances of Class A, B or C regulation. It is the prescription that validates the legal possession and use of the relevant medications. Where a prescription is not issued to a person who is using someone else's medication or has bought strong painkillers on the black market, then that is managed in the same way as illegal drugs. The EWCM will help identify the nature of the shop floor culture with regard to illegally used prescribed medications.

Other countermeasures need to be considered for the management of legally prescribed medications, including confidential self-referral mechanisms, EAP, reasonable adjustments and confidential reporting of impairment from prescribed medications.

This book and the EWCM help with these processes.

Smoking in the workplace, like society, has to be regulated and restricted. Smoking has its own dependency issues and treatment/intervention protocols. There is a need in the workplace to cater for those who have a desire or dependency to smoke. Countermeasures put in place to restrict smoking areas or eliminate them altogether develop a workplace culture of:

- *How do we get around this?*
- *Where can we go to smoke undetected in the workplace?*
- *Where is it safe?*
- *What are the consequences of being caught?*
- *Where is the risk of fire reduced, and so on?*

Smoking cessation campaigns are an obvious answer to helping employees' health and wellbeing and also reduce the conflict between the smoker and the non-smoker. Nicotine replacement therapy sponsored by the employer is a great initiative for those companies that invest in people. The social aspect of smoking has been greatly impacted by it being banned in the workplace, restaurants, bars and other social meeting areas. The workplace needs to identify the nature of the workplace smoking culture. Over the years there has been a gradual decline in smokers; there still exists, however, a black market economy of illegal cheap tobacco circulating in society and the workplace, which also has to be managed. Just like alcohol, tobacco is generally a legal substance and therefore defers to policy application associated with proactive countermeasures. *Unless you know the nature of the problem how can you best manage it?*

This book and EWCM will help this process.
The *Drug User Disorder Information Test (DUDIT)* was developed as a psychological and physiological process to assess the nature of the individual who had a drug dependency issue, whether illegal drugs or legally prescribed drugs. Some of the DUDIT questions for a workplace assessment were not appropriate, nor did they have any relevance to identify a general workplace problem. The full range of DUDIT questions does, however, have a role to play once an employee self-refers a dependency and is subsequently required to be referred or self-refer into a controlled clinical intervention as outlined in the EAP chapter. The workplace demands on the DUDIT revolve around identifying the scale of the problem collectively and then individually once an EAP is made available within a workplace SAMP and POT. The demographics of drugs vary with the predominance of the drug dealer network and the predominance of the drug being pushed, with cocaine and cannabis being the most predominant at the moment. Drug demographics also exist with regard to an individual's needs for stimulants such as amphetamines in certain sectors or job-specific markers where conditions are challenging or shift durations are both exhausting and protracted. Other social drugs such as Ecstasy, spice, synthetic drugs and so-called festival drugs come along from time to time as and when the need to party or a culture around them develops. Anabolic steroids are more of an issue in the gym and body enhancement areas, and the other problems created by the use of anabolic steroids are the issues that have to be managed in the workplace.

The EWCM was designed to expose these and other issues within a workplace environment where criminal and civil legislations are constantly applied or threatened to the business owners and those who manage the workplace's day-to-day activity. The variety of legislations influence the manner by which policies and procedures are developed, prioritized and managed. *How can you deal with a problem if you don't know*

- *What is it?*
- *Where is it?*

- *When is it happening?*
- *Who is involved?*
- *What is the scale of the problem, pre- and post-EWCM?*
- *What are the consequences of failing to comply?*
- *Whom do those consequences apply to?*

This book and the EWCM will help with these processes and obligations.

The *Alcohol User Disorder Information Test (AUDIT)*, like the DUDIT, was designed for the psychological/physiological and clinical intervention of those who had, in this case, an alcohol dependency. Just like in the DUDIT, some of the AUDIT questions needed to be eliminated or modified to best reflect the needs of the employer in the management of alcohol misuse, either in the workplace or with regard to the effects of alcohol on the employee on arrival at the workplace. Too many companies apply the guidelines of the English Road Traffic Act to workplace alcohol counter-measures. As a result of devolution in the UK, the alcohol legal drink drive limit cut-off in England, Wales and Northern Ireland is 35 micrograms per 100 millilitres of breath, but in Scotland it is 22 micrograms. In the Republic of Ireland and Europe the cut-off is even less and can depend on age as well as profession; e.g. truck drivers' cut-offs are half of those who drive private vehicles.

Too many companies apply a blood alcohol cut-off in a policy when they cannot take blood and are using breath test devices that measure evidential deep lung breath. The term evidential breath-test device (EBD) can be applied only to breath test devices used for prosecution, not the screening devices used in the workplace or the type of approved devices that allow a constable in uniform a power of arrest and detention, and then test on an EBD back at the police station. So, beware in your application of breath testing and how you manage it, especially when setting a limit below the relevant legal drink driving limit. If your policy is set below a legal driving limit, remember, you are dealing with a legal substance, as for tobacco.

The EWCM can also be applied to identify functioning alcoholics as well as non-functioning alcoholics, although the latter are more obvious to a trained person. As alcohol is legal there is a need to understand the very nature of the workplace culture around alcohol and its impact into the work-place, the result of which should help you decide what your company cut-off should be.

This book and the EWCM will help in this process and a great many others.
Criminality and whistle-blowing in the workplace is an ongoing problem
that is both varied and can have devastating consequences to the company's
ability to survive and continue trading. The basic theft of raw material, finished product, point of delivery issues, product diversion/hijacking, fraud and
embezzlement, intimidation, drug dealing and so on all have an impact on
the employee, the employer and very often the local community. The infiltration of organized crime allied to opportunist local crime are all negatives to a
business. There are proactive and reactive countermeasures to be brought to
bear in the management or identification of trends around shrinkage, discrep-
ancy reporting and so on. Without a doubt, the route to identifying a great
deal of workplace criminality is the employees themselves. Many companies
have internal whistle-blowing protocols; these are, however, mistrusted generally, as outlined earlier. Few companies employ an independent provider
to respond to and report on workplace whistle-blowing. Many companies
employ very expensive audit process providers for compliance and physical
audit of accounts and inventory, all fall short of internal routes to criminal
information gathering and processing.

The EWCM is a confidential route to discovering some of those issues
not normally discussed openly. The freedom an employee has within the
EWCM for whistle-blowing is massive. The identification of the culture
around employees' attitudes to reporting or informing the company about
issues that can cost them their business and their jobs should not be avoided.
The management team needs to have the details of the EWCM to help direct
their proactive and reactive processes across multiple subjects.

The EWCM in particular will help in this process, as will the content of this
book.

Chapter summary

Each of the above topics contained in the EWCM is a formula that will help
a company manage its business, its employees and its expectations. While
in the early days of development the EWCM was dedicated to substance
and alcohol misuse management there was a clear and natural progression
to direct it towards other topics around support to the employee and the
employer.

Do

1. Consider the workplace culture map at the start of planning for a workplace substance misuse programme, especially during the 90-day amnesty period.
2. Use it on a regular basis to measure your progression.
3. Use it to measure how much the employees are engaging within your and their expectations.
4. Consider it as a management tool in identifying best practice as well as bad practice.
5. Use to look inward as well as outward at the company's overall efficiency and ultimately sustainability.
6. Communicate its complete findings post completion, warts and all.

Do not

1. Keep the findings to a select few. Remember this package is about employee/employer engagement; make it so.
2. Ignore the findings. They will be the measure by which you will be judged as an employer and ultimately a manager of many possible solutions to identified problems.
3. Sit on the results for too long. Confrontation for identified problems will be exaggerated by inactivity to ignoring the obvious need.
4. Ignore the proactive input of the employees who may have identified one or more initiatives that they can actively become involved in or manage themselves.
5. Think that an annual EWCM is the only route to engaging with the workforce. There are other initiatives and processes that should run parallel with EWCM.
6. Use the findings for operational weakness as a disciplinary tool. In many situations you will find it an effective identification of the need for specific training at all levels.

7

Workplace substance misuse investigations

Introduction

The investigation of workplace substance misuse is alluded to in various parts of this book. If we are not investigating the person it's the workplace; if it's not the workplace it's the policy; if it's not the policy it's the toxicology or testing programme and so on. Illegal and black market substance activities have a direct correlation to criminality. It's the management of criminality in the workplace that has to have an overt and covert capability, usually supported by a zero tolerance approach when detected. The overriding factor is the *zero-tolerance* approach to criminality, which has to be made very clear in every workplace to every employee, contractor and visitor to the business either via specific policies or terms and conditions (T&Cs) of employment, induction protocols, etc. Employers cannot be seen to allow criminality to be conducted, condoned or go unpunished. Employees who come to work in an environment where intimidation and criminality go unchallenged will always look to the employer to protect them and the business.

When developing corporate or commercial strategies there are many who feel they have the investigative ability to produce evidence that is sufficient either in the balance of probability for civil courts or beyond all reasonable doubt for criminal courts. Investigations begin around a range of situations, such as:

- Suspicion that something is about to happen.
- Something is happening.
- Something has happened.

- There is a need to prevent something from happening.
- There is a need to allow something to happen.
- Loss prevention, detection and recovery.

In all situations it is better for the investigator to have access to those suspects who are involved in any situation before they are dismissed. All too often, HR and others will take a decision to dismiss a person or persons without conducting an enhanced extraction protocol so that the company can investigate situations that lead to the need to dismiss as opposed to suspend someone for further investigation. While the main suspect has been identified there is very often collusion with work colleagues, contractors and supply chain. The loss of control over the main suspect(s) makes it harder to detect and identify the who, what, when and why necessity in its entirety. Never underestimate the volume of potential witnesses that are willing to come forward once a person is suspended. This also applies to the subsequent structured dismissal. An experienced corporate/commercial investigator is not just trained in interview techniques and evidence gathering. There are other areas of expertise, some of which are:

- Forensic examination of systems, documents, policies and processes.
- The presentation of evidence and management of witnesses for civil and criminal courts.
- The management of witnesses, including through the tribunal court procedure where witness preparation is very important.
- The investigation of criminal actions where the police have no expertise or are restricted by geographic boundaries or jurisdiction issues.
- The ability to conduct covert and overt operations on and away from site, or in other countries.
- The ability to install and manage undercover employees into the workplace.
- The ability to risk assess and audit all manner of processes including physical security countermeasures, operational audits, financial audits and risk exposure through goods and raw material in or out/manufacture/distribution of finished product/point of delivery failings/managing zero rated stock or returns and much more.
- The ability to conduct covert surveillance whether physical or electronic.
- In the global arena the ability to investigate or set standards around:
  1. Money laundering activities.

2. Antiterrorist activities/infiltration into a business, usually in association with 1 above.
3. Organized international and local crime infiltration into the business.
4. The infiltration of drugs into the workplace nationally and internationally, especially via company shipping routes.
5. Investigate and prepare counterfeit product countermeasures.
6. Investigate product diversion/highjacking.
7. Investigate product contamination around food and drink.
8. Investigate and prevent patent infringement and brand integrity.
9. Industrial espionage with regard to research and development and/or labour dispute sabotage.
10. Investigating the usual and regular events of fraud, theft, embezzlement, bribery and corruption and so on.
11. VIP insertion and extraction protocols, especially into and out of risk areas.
12. Industrial dispute investigation and mediation.

Above are some of the areas that an experienced corporate and commercial investigator will be called on to manage or advise. It makes no difference whether the investigation is a multimillion-dollar fraud or a straightforward local offence, the application of investigative skills and principals are generally the same. White-collar crime is just as prevalent as blue-collar crime. *The debate is, which impacts the workplace the most?*

The overriding factor for the corporate investigator, as stated, was getting access to the issues and the persons responsible before they were dismissed and lost to being properly interviewed and processed. Too many companies deal with an incident to get rid of it within their day-to-day business operations as soon as they possibly can. They do not consider the other fallout of criminality that has as yet gone undetected. They believe that if they make a report to the relevant law enforcement agency it will be responded to quickly. When it comes to crimes that transgress international and national boundaries the police are not too excited about coming forward and will argue budget, not enough resources, geographic restriction and, as stated, jurisdiction. Even for the simplest situations their response can be very much protracted by the normal day-to-day services they provide into the community and the myriad of other demands not often seen by the public.

Example

There is a need to investigate a multimillion-dollar fraud which had complications in the UK, Brazil and Europe. The local UK police would not send the fraud squad directly to such issues, and the following then ensued:

1. Local police were called and asked to send a fraud squad detective to take the case on from a UK prosecution perspective.
2. The constabulary refused and sent a local uniformed officer to record a crime on the relevant documentation, standard operating procedures for UK police response. The officer had no clue as to what he was recording or what would be recorded into UK crime statistics. This is handled by another department. The basic crime report was taken for classification and allocation to other investigative departments.
3. Once the crime was processed some weeks later the local police force sent a detective sergeant and detective constable to investigate, after many requests for urgency. The attending detectives said they had no clue what we were describing but agreed a criminal offence(s) had been committed and that the fraud squad would have to be notified as they had not been trained in financial pushdowns, international law and banking, etc. – a point made clear to the constabulary on the first report.
4. Some *months* later the fraud squad attended over a period of 3 days to gather what needed to be done to compile a report to senior officers and to upgrade their own knowledge.
5. Some months after that they came back and said they had been in touch with the Serious Fraud Office (SFO) as they did not have enough money in the force budget or enough spare capacity for officers to be released to investigate a large multimillion-dollar crime that was for them, complicated by company governance and multiple departmental evidence gathering across three countries.
6. Some weeks later the SFO responded to say the crime was below their new investigative threshold and deferred the investigation back to the local constabulary.
7. By the time the force had come back to reluctantly accept the case, the corporate investigator had conducted all internal investigations and prepared a Section 10 (Crown Court) committal file, processed all evidence and gathered all documentary evidence and identified all evidence trails.

8. It took the force another 6 months to arrest the offender and another 2 years to get him to Crown Court and a subsequent conviction with a custodial sentence in excess of 3 years.

9. From the point of arrest to the actual court date there were myriad other issues in the collection of evidence not used, change of the police investigating officer and company departmental staff, many of whom were dismissed for failing to comply with corporate governance.

Throughout this whole process there were internal investigations galore and accusations levied towards the well-known external compliance and audit companies that missed the theft and fraud in its entirety.

While this situation may seem extreme, it happens all the time, and the same principles occur, just on lesser or grander scales. There are two issues to consider at the start of any internal investigation:

1. *Do you as a company want to prosecute if the evidence is sufficient?*
2. *Do you as a company not want the investigation detail delivered into the public domain and therefore kept confidential and away from public courts?*

These two issues are commercial decisions for the company and its officers to take into account. In order to do that, the company and its officers need to know the full extent and every aspect of the investigation's result and any remedial recommendations that are identified and reported on for immediate action. Where possible, a professional investigator should be called in before any employee is formally dismissed.

In Chapter 1, I made reference to two case studies. One was specifically derived from a comprehensive risk assessment of all of the company's processes and the specific input from an existing undercover employee which took the investigation to a new level. The other was the reverse, we conducted the risk assessment, had a great many unanswered questions and so placed an undercover employee into the workplace to flush out where the issues were manifest across a multiple product manufacturer.

With regard to substance misuse investigation and its correlation to criminality, there are a number of approaches to investigating the subject in the workplace. Just as in the two case studies of Chapter 1, a highly specialized undercover employee can be placed into position for reasons other than substance misuse and distribution. I have instigated and micro-managed a great many undercover operations, in 95% of which drug misuse/distribution was found first and foremost.

So, what are the investigative methodologies we can bring to the workplace to identify and eliminate substance misuse and its correlation to the wider subject of criminality and workplace intimidation? Many are visible in this book, situations such as:

1. Pre-employment drug testing, to stop the problem from getting into the workplace in the first place. It is much more costly and difficult to detect and manage it out than it is to prevent it becoming a problem.

2. If you use an employment agency, ensure you apply your testing programme to the Service Level Agreement, and where they send you potential staff who test positive, reverse the charges to the recruitment agency. Employment agencies need to engage full due diligence in the recruitment of temporary or full-time staff.

3. A robust workplace substance misuse policy and Programme of Testing for existing employees, contractors and application of relevant criminal and civil legislations, as outlined in Chapter 4.

4. The Electronic Workplace Culture Map (EWCM) which will, along with other topics, help you identify and manage substance misuse and other negatives out of the business in a single visit. In the free text box of each section of the culture map there is also the capability for employee whistle-blowing. This is a cheaper option to the undercover employee scenario. It should, however, be a rapid response platform for the investigator to take action with and on behalf of the company.

5. For those companies that conduct large-scale drug testing, you should have the means to conduct an intelligence analysis of the positive test results. There is a significant amount of information to be gathered from a combination of the toxicology report and the construction of the consent and chain of custody documentation. With our own TOX247 design collection documents we specifically add location, shift pattern and job description to our documentation. This leads us to conduct regular and proactive reporting investigations that will allow for the identification of hot spots in the following areas:
    *   Which is the predominant drug.
    *   Which shift pattern or location has a hot spot for a specific drug or more positives than another shift or location.
    *   Which department has the most positives.
    *   Which location, in multisite operations, is above the company norm.
    *   Which person(s), pre-employment, agency, contractor, profession, etc.

6. As a result of the above information there are four issues to consider:
   (a) Having identified the hot spots by drug, location and shift, let's consider installing an undercover employee to flush out the problem.
   (b) Conduct a workplace culture mapping exercise.
   (c) Conduct for-cause, rapid result back to laboratory testing across the relevant shift, department or location.
   (d) If not already in place activate a 24/7 whistle-blowing programme.

7. When applying these methodologies, there are a number of other distinctions/target information:
   (a) Identifying the user
   (b) Identifying the dealer
   (c) When
   (d) Where
   (e) How
   (f) Why
   (g) The local drug demographics where the problem exists

We have already discussed the management of each of these situations directly or indirectly in this book. The level of intimidation applied by the workplace dealer on and away from company premises when associating with employees is immense. The weakness or vulnerability of some individuals intimidated by the dealer is very noticeable when they are interviewed. You will find the reaction from other employees is only positive and supportive for the actions you will take as a company in removing this *hidden threat* from the workplace and ultimately its management/exposure in the local communities. Law enforcement will always welcome new intelligence that may already be part of a larger investigation or simply completely unknown to them.

Example

At a particular UK retail distribution centre multiple drug dealers and users were active within a particular shift pattern. A shop floor informant came forward and was further cultivated to firm-up and expand on the thin evidence originally provided to the management team, who needed guidance as to how to best expose what was going on. Once the corporate investigator had validated all relevant information, action was planned and subsequently taken by:

- Removing the suspects from the workplace.
- Closing down toilets post search and preventing their use.
- Conducting searches utilizing local police drug dogs against the suspected person, lockers, vehicles and around the general workplace.

- Conducting for-cause testing of the suspects, all tested positive.
- Conducting witness and criminal interviewing by using contemporaneous investigation notes; see below.
- Dismissal and immediate arrest of a number of employees.
- Suspension of a number of employees, mostly from information of the dealers who made lists of their client-base within the workforce.

The combination of overt and covert measures taken in this situation meant that it was clear to the whole shift what had been activated by the site management team being advised by a specialist investigator.

At a debrief of the large shift pattern there was a resounding round of applause and a chorus of 'About time too'. The management team moved immediately to a position of power, fully supported by the majority of employees during further management initiatives. A wide range of criminality and substance misuse issues were uncovered and managed out of the business, with the blessing of the on-site union representatives. Above all the employees felt more comfortable in communicating to the management team any further suspicions they had, based on the fact they had confidence in what had been conducted by the company.

In many workplace drug and criminality investigations there is a need to identify the level of confidence and communication that exists between the management team and the workforce. That is always best examined during any witness/accused interview process pre- and post-investigation and should be part of an investigation checklist.

Principles for interviewing an accused employee

When it comes to interviewing employees for suspected criminal offences or other gross misconduct scenarios, there are many trains of thought on which the employee should be formally cautioned before questions are asked. When I say cautioned I mean the statement in the UK:

'You do not have to say anything, but it may harm your defence if you do not mention something when questioned that you later rely on in evidence. Anything you do say may be given in evidence.'

In the USA it's the Miranda Act that is considered, and around the world there are many other variations of formal interviewing. Be sure wherever you operate that any evidence you gather can be applied where necessary into criminal or civil litigation and your actions do not negate its submission.

The argument in the UK was that although the interview was not conducted within the rules of the Police and Criminal Evidence Act (PACE), the caution allowed the interview notes to be put into the police prosecution file under 'Unused Material' and as such disclosed to the defence.

I tend to disregard this approach and use the UK's Advisory, Conciliation and Arbitration Service (ACAS) guidelines which should be put to any employee being interviewed where he or she may be disciplined, lose their job or possibly arrested. That statement is:

'So that you can be fairly judged, we ask that you answer all questions fairly, do you understand?'

This is the same approach to take when interviewing someone during a disciplinary situation or other scenarios which require investigations that are not criminal in nature, but an accurate record of the event is required. The reason for this approach is that for employment law you have made the employee's position very clear to them. If you are planning to have them arrested it is much better that you are in a position to dismiss them prior to arrest. The last thing you need is a situation where a serving employee is in custody or on remand and still not dismissed and no right to attend any workplace appeal, if it is done in their absence. There have been many situations where employees have been dismissed for very serious offences, the police have not responded immediately and the employee has then gone on the run from police prosecution by leaving not just the area but also the country in which they live.

The manner of the interview needs to be compliant with the company's own guidelines around the discipline code and the company's governance on the subject. There are a variety of situations that can evolve from the disciplinary process and these can include:

- Solicitors/legal representatives of the accused are not invited to these internal discipline procedures.
- The accused should, however, be offered the opportunity for a work colleague or union representative to be present to ensure fair play without intimidation. The employee's witness is not there to answer questions on behalf of the employee.
- Any person being a witness for the accused must have had no part to play or be suspect in the same incident as the accused.

- A non-workplace friend is a last resort as you need to know their background, especially where there has been collusion off site around the sale of stolen company goods.
- The interviewer where possible should have a witness of their own, either from the company or another experienced interviewer.
- Conduct the interview in an appropriate location and an appropriate manner. The accused person should be told they can leave at any time during the interview while being reminded they will be judged on both their own and the company's evidence. They should also be told they can suspend the interview at any time for a break or other appropriate necessity. Remember, as an investigator or company you have no power to detain an employee against their wishes.
- Always be prepared to record the interview by way of contemporaneous note taking (notes made at the time: write the question down and then write the answer down). Some investigators provide double tape deck recording devices. Whichever method is used the accused should have the opportunity to:
  (a) Read or review the interview content.
  (b) Where contemporaneous notes are taken ensure at all times the interviewers details and accused/witness signatures, names, etc. are legible.
  (c) Any alterations and crossing out of writing is still made legible and initialed by the accused.
  (d) Make sure each written answer made by the accused is initialed so that nothing else can be added after the finish of the interview.
  (e) Make sure the bottom of each interview page is signed by the interviewer, the accused and all witnesses present. On occasion some witnesses refuse to sign; make sure an endorsement is made to that effect and the accused initials or signs the addition.
  (f) Make sure that any spare space on the last page is rendered unusable by putting a line through it and have the interviewer and accused sign across the spare space.
  (g) Before that spare space is covered off there is a need to write the following paragraph having already said to the accused:

  I now want you to read the questions and answers you have given, if you agree they are correct I want you to initial each answer and sign the bottom of each page. You can correct alter or add anything you wish. You may also register any complaint about the conduct of this interview.

This approach eliminates all subsequent complaints produced at any appeal or litigation about the manner of the interview and its subsequent content.

(h) Always ensure you have entered the time the interview commenced, any breaks taken and when the interview was completed.

Principles for interviewing a witness

When interviewing a witness always remember they may become an accused as a result of what they say. If they are a colleague or a manager, they may have actually unwittingly have become involved in the accused's activities. There is often a need to examine the possibility of hidden agendas between the witness/accused and vice versa. Additionally, you cannot force anyone to become a witness. It must be a completely voluntary situation, and the last thing you need is a hostile witness examination. There is as much thought put into witness interviewing as there is to the interview of an accused. As outlined in one of the points above there is also a need to prepare a witness should they be required to present evidence internally, at a tribunal or criminal case.

A witness statement is different from a witness interview. The interview can be conducted in the workplace or in the case of a whistle-blower off site and away from the eyes and ears of the workplace. The witness interview is the preparation prior to committing to paper and additional or direct evidence against an accused person. The witness interview should be a less formal process of covering off a list of questions and proof around the answers. The witness interview and the taking of a statement can be days apart. The statement does not have to immediately follow the interview, and it's very often good practice to conduct a number of witness interviews and conduct other investigative enquiries before you commit to paper and or judge the credibility of the witness. It is always a good decision to keep notes of what questions have been asked of the witness(es). It may be the only evidence you have to work with.

Before taking the witness statement, you need to remind them that:

- The information they provided needs to be accurate.
- Where possible any supporting documents for their evidence and particular to them should be evidenced in their statement and an evidence number allocated.

- The information needs to be honest and in their own words.
- They need to be reminded their evidence may be challenged.
- They need to be reminded that if it can potentially used in a criminal prosecution and that will bring into play other issues around perjury or other country-specific applications that will be pointed out by the law enforcement agency appointed.

With regard to workplace drug dealing and substance misuse issues it is good practice to drug test the workplace witness(es) in the same manner as the accused (wide- and/or narrow-window test). This test should be completed before any witness interviewing/ statement taking is conducted. It is not, however, critical to progressing the investigation. Part of checking the credibility of the witness is to ask a direct question such as 'Are you currently misusing any illegal or legal substances?' If local law enforcement agencies are engaged during the investigation let them know what has been done so far with regard to any witness or accused testing. This will also need to be allowed for in the T&Cs of employment and the disclosure of employee details within General Data Protection Regulation (GDPR, UK) or any other data protection guidelines relevant to the country in which you operate.

In the event a quantity of drugs is seized or surrendered in the workplace investigation the law around possession of that drug is that it should be locked away and the police informed. You can also take it straight to the police station (UK) to deliver it within the guidelines of the UK Misuse of Drugs Act.

Do

1. Record the circumstances it came into your possession.
2. Record who was involved in its recovery/surrender.
3. Have another witness with you whenever you can in its receipt and locking away.
4. Get a disclaimer from the person it has been seized from.
5. Take a photograph of it.
6. If the police cannot attend immediately do make an appointment as soon as possible to take it to the police station to be surrendered to that lawful authority.

Do not

1. Taste it, snort it, touch it or open any wrapping under any circumstances. You do not know what it is. It may be a very toxic or poisonous compound.
2. Keep it in an insecure draw or any secure/insecure holding situation for more than 24–48 hours. If the police cannot come to you, you should go to them and take a witness with you.
3. Keep it in your personal possession or car, at all. It only goes with you when you and a witness go with it to the police station on a pre-arranged visit.
4. Keep it and present it to the accused in any workplace interview. Drug seizures need to be analysed before any interview takes place; by all means ask the accused what it is. There is no quality control in crime; it may or may not be a drug, it may or may not be dangerous. Let the lab sort out exactly what it is. Accused parties when shown their own drugs again have been known to grab and eat the evidence.

Investigation is a prove /disprove scenario to a very wide range of topics that will invoke a commercial decision or a prosecution. When investigating the infiltration of drugs into the workplace and the workforce, the *Toxicology Report* is an essential tool to

- The company and its management team
- The investigator
- The employee
- The potential rehabilitation/removal process

Chapter 4 contains a copy of an anonymous toxicology report for you to review. In Chapter 5 we discussed the importance of the toxicology results of the donor within the Employee Assistance Programme (EAP). There is a need to now look at how the toxicology report is of use to the company and the designated investigator. The toxicology report will outline certain details about the individual user and the overall assessment of the situation of substance misuse across the company.

Example

Cocaine paste is an importation drug for UK resale. So, if we seize cocaine paste in the workplace or society the user and the potential dealer are closer to the source of importation. This places the workplace investigation into a different perspective. Questions are then asked as to how we get closer to that importation organization and the need to ensure it is not the company shipping routes that have been compromised.

While cocaine paste is not a specific compound for the toxicology report, it is more of a pre-use preparation that rings alarm bells to the investigator, as does black tar heroin and cutting agents such as fentanyl and car-fentanyl.

When it comes to the individual toxicology report there is a need to examine from it:

1. *Is the donor a single drug misuser and to what extent is the toxicology report reporting above the minimum legal cut-off?*
2. *Is the donor a cocktail drug misuser and again to what level above the legal cut-off?*
3. *Which test medium was used to detect the drug, head or body hair, fingernail clippings, saliva or urine?* Each has their own characteristics when metabolizing a drug metabolite or cross-reactive compound.
4. If the result is very high above cut-off there is a need to consider questions around the possibility that on-site dealing is occurring.
5. *Is the drug identified as a repeat drug across other workplace positives?*
6. *Is the drug an unusual drug when looking at existing drug demographics within the company?*

These are a few of the considerations when examining laboratory positives and the impact they may have in the workplace. They are some of the reasons why drug testing has a larger part to play in any company-structured Programme of Testing and policy development.

As an expert witness and corporate investigator who has evolved specifically from the field of national and international provision, I have had the opportunity to review and rewrite hundreds of workplace substance and alcohol misuse policies and deliver a wide variety of workplace training programmes. Each of the chapters in this book has important elements to play in any company's approach to managing its business and its employees.

The chapters can be considered collectively or applied individually. I am going to end this chapter with questions as opposed to the Do and Do Not situations. Some of these questions I ask when looking to help an employee examine an unfair dismissal scenario, some when meeting a client for the first time, some to examine the legality and construction of a substance misuse policy that needs to have a Programme of Testing and EAP integral to it, nearly all are relevant to whether your profession is:

*   Health & safety professional
*   HR/personnel development professional

- Legal professional
- Insurance provider
- Occupational health professional
- Operations director
- Manager or other leadership capacity
- Procurement professional
- Compliance professional
- Independent professional in any of the named professions
- An employer
- An employee
- Any unidentified discipline

For those companies that are conducting workplace substance and alcohol misuse countermeasures:

1. *Is your policy fit for purpose?*
2. *Have you had your policy reviewed by a specialist provider with a track record of excellence?*
3. *Are your consent mechanisms and training records up-to-date with GDPR or other regulation/statutory requirements?*
4. *Is your policy legally enforceable/defensible?*
5. *Which statutory requirements need to be considered for your sector?*
6. *Is the policy up-to-date within a wide variety of current legislations and scientific developments?*
7. *When was the policy last reviewed, by whom and what were their qualifications to do so?*
8. *Who wrote the policy, what training have they had and what is their expertise in administering what is a very complicated subject?*
9. *Does your policy reflect the Programme of Testing you have or are about to implement?*
10. *Does your policy rely on presumptive consent as opposed to actual consent and proof of consent?*
11. *Have you properly implemented all pre-policy protocols such as amnesty periods, consultation, GDPR protocols?*
12. *Have you provided an appropriate Employee Assistance Programme (EAP) that is designed to help self-referrals for substance and alcohol misuse/dependency issues?*
13. *Is the EAP designed with enrolment, compliance and removal criteria?*
14. *Is the EAP structured for the examination of relevant clinical history, unmet needs, treatment profile and, more importantly, a treatment outcome?*

What are the principles behind the creation of the policy, such as:

1. *Why do we need a policy, legally, morally or imposed?*
2. *Whom does it apply to?*
3. *When does it apply?*
4. *Under which circumstances are we going to apply it?*
5. *Which consequences of breaching the policy are being applied and under which circumstances?*
6. *Has the policy been enforced on you or are you enforcing it on other third parties?*
7. *What training have company directors and managers had with regard to their culpability or responsibility with regard to the policy and its ramifications?*
8. *Who is managing and/or administering the policy and the Programme of Testing, and are they trained to do so?*
9. *Is the policy and Programme of Testing the same thing and can one exist without the other?*

With regard to the construction of the policy itself an assessment needs to be made to examine:

1. *Does the policy have too much general information in it that is not policy or is being applied as policy and therefore not enforceable at all?*
2. *Is general information necessary in policy?*
3. *Have we put any criminal and civil legislations into the policy. If so, why and why did we leave other relevant legislations out?*
4. *Is the policy comprehensive enough to protect the company and its employees?*
5. *Is our Programme of Testing explained or identified in the policy and what are the consequences of failing to comply or providing a positive back to laboratory result?*
6. *Where do we place our standard operating procedures and instructions for the donor and collector to be aware of?*
7. *Have we put anything in the policy that exposes us to non-relevant legal challenge?*

Other questions that should be asked by an employee and certainly by the employer who has dismissed an employee under the substance and alcohol misuse programme:

1. *Has the policy been legally applied to me or by me?*
2. *Have testing procedures been complied with?*

3. *Is the toxicology report accurate and does it contain sufficient evidence for a tribunal or criminal case?*
4. *What information can or should I have or provide with regard to my test or my testing programme?*
5. *Have I been dismissed or have dismissed someone illegally?*

The complete content of this book has been designed to answer many of these questions and many more that can be asked. This chapter in particular highlights some of the dark arts but by no means all of them.

My desire is that you are able to use the contents of this book with confidence in the way you develop your own approach to the management of substance and alcohol misuse in the workplace and also manage the correlation of substance misuse to criminality regardless of which country you live in and work.

Index

enforcement 2, 3, 48, 109, 175, 181, 196, 197
England 10, 19, 20, 94, 108, 119, 166, 181, 182, 201
ephedrine 90
equality 62, 75
Equality Act 2010 111
escalation 10, 26, 92, 177
espionage 206
Europe 4, 131, 201, 207
evidential breath-test device (EBD) 68, 201
EWCM see Electronic Workplace Culture Map (EWCM)
examination 48, 49, 52, 55, 57, 62–63, 70, 73, 82, 91, 156, 177, 179, 189, 197, 205, 214, 218
excessive alcohol consumption 117, 140
ex-offenders 5
expectations 89, 156, 189, 202, 203
expense 11, 67, 85, 101, 188, 202
experience 1, 2, 39, 80, 82, 97, 158, 187
expertise 84, 205, 218
extended brief intervention (EBI) 169
extraction protocols 205–206

face-to-face contact 137
failure to communicate 44
failure to comply 76, 91, 130, 132, 136, 171, 201, 208, 219
fair assessment 156
fair play 212
fair presentation 11, 17, 92, 94, 106, 148
fake diversion kits 79
false positives/negatives 63, 71
families 9, 37, 93, 95, 96, 102; family context 155; family environment 3, 40; family members 3, 21, 35; family situation 90
fatal overdose 28, 32
fatal road traffic accidents 2
fatal submission 87
fatigue 79

FDA 12
fentanyl 28, 29, 217
festivals 96, 200
fiduciary duty 7, 8, 14, 18, 39, 87, 94, 106, 137, 159, 165, 171, 182, 198
finance departments 189
financial audits 205
financial impact 177
fingernail clipping, testing 20, 48, 57, 61, 64, 73, 75, 109, 124, 133, 147, 155, 217
fitness for work 8, 20, 21, 95, 115, 122, 163, 174
fitness to drive 8
flight and cabin crew 68
fluids, testing 66, 67, 73, 74, 99, 109, 133, 134, 136, 140, 147
Flunitrazepam 181
follow-up 121, 126
forensic examination 205
formal training 4, 82–83, 101
four-phase approach see four-phase modular approach
four-phase modular approach 101, 103; four-phase modular structure 82
fraud 3, 202, 206–208
frequency 111, 154, 166
full-pay suspension 52, 56, 65, 71
functioning addicts 27, 141, 165–166, 172, 175, 201

gabapentin 49, 54
gamma-hydroxybutyric acid (GHB) 60
gases 34, 60, 108
GDPR see general data protection regulation (GDPR)
general data protection regulation (GDPR) 12, 18, 19, 88–89, 113, 150, 159, 215, 218
GHB see gamma-hydroxybutyric acid (GHB)
glues 34, 108
gouching out 1